Arkansas Dairy Bars

Neat Eats & Cool Treats

Arkansas
Dairy Bars
Neat Eats & Cool Treats

Kat Robinson

TONTI
PRESS

Published by Tonti Press
Little Rock, Arkansas
Copyright © 2021 by Kat Robinson. All rights reserved.

First published October 2021

Manufactured in the United States of America

ISBN: 978-1-952547-05-8

Library of Congress Control Number: 2021946567

Softcover release November 2021

ISBN: 978-1-952547-04-1

The author accepted no compensation for inclusion of any restaurant in this book. All photographs of food consist of edible, real food not enhanced with photographic tricks, manipulation or fakery. Photographs were taken by the author, except in cases of screenshots from the program bearing the same name as this book from cinematographer Jeff Dailey, and of historic photographs largely gathered from the location in which they were taken. Additional photography provided by Grav Weldon.

The concept of this book was sparked during the COVID-19 pandemic of 2020-2021. All efforts were made to safely research the subject while maintaining social distance and wearing personal protective devices.

To John Fulton
and Leslie Luther-Fulton

Adventure awaits!

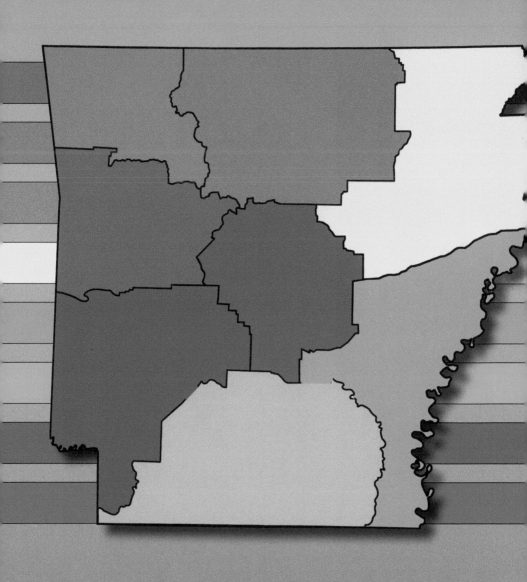

INTRODUCTION

Dairy bars: when I mention this type of restaurant to people who don't live in Arkansas, I often get a blank stare. In other places, these joints are called milk bars. And – in other places – they aren't quite as common as they are here in The Natural State. But they're a marvelous way to feed your nostalgia, even in the risky COVID-19 age.

Back in January 2021, I was looking for my next project. I had spent time during the pandemic writing cookbooks instead of the travel guides for which I am well known. But, like many, I was itching to get out and about again and resume my normal life – normal, for me, being visiting, researching, and sharing the stories of our state's fine dining establishments.

My partner and I were out one Saturday after-noon delivering books. I wanted ice cream, and so did he, so we stopped in at a place I knew – a restaurant that didn't even have a street sign. That place was Mel's Dairy Bar in Malvern. It's south of downtown on U.S. Highway 67, a little yellow building from whence ice cream and massive burgers come.

It was while I was enjoying a caramel shake that the idea popped into my head: dairy bars – by their own natural construction – are likely the best pre-pared restaurants for pandemic times. Orders are through a window, as are pick-ups. Social distancing can be maintained safely. And there's a nostalgic kick to be considered.

I awoke the next morning with the idea to create a book on the subject and got busy researching the state's dairy bars. I was quite surprised to find that the model I had thought about was indeed working well: of the state's 95 dairy bars around in 2019, some 94 of them were still in operation.

So, I traveled safely, wearing my personal protection, and visited each of these locations. I sampled all sorts of fare – from remarkable butterscotch sundaes at Lion's Den Drive In in Clarendon and the steak fingers at the Lighthouse Drive-In in Wickes to dipped cones at Portia's Dairy King and righteous burgers at Sheridan's Yellow Jacket Drive-In – and started building this book.

When Arkansas PBS decided it was time to create another Arkansas food program, "Arkansas Dairy Bars" seemed like the perfect entry. Over the course of three weeks in late March and early April, cinematographer Jeff Dailey and I traveled to a host of different locations across this marvelous state, recording the stories of the dairy bars selected and the people who work in them.

On August 19, 2021, "Arkansas Dairy Bars: Neat Eats and Cool Treats" debuted on Arkansas PBS, sharing stories from so many of these dairy bars. The show included the stories of so many locations and the people who worked there, the dishes on the menus, and the histories around each one. Of course, they say the book is always better than the movie, so I'll let you be the judge of that.

At the time of this writing, we're still coping with the global pandemic. But each of the dairy bars mentioned in this book continues to thrive. And, a happy surprise - as this book was going to press, we discovered that the one location that had closed during the pandemic, the Timbo Dairy Bar in the Timbo community, had come back as Brad and Dad's Drive In. The location had previously held the distinction of that name before, and it's being run by cousins of the Timbo Dairy Bar owners. After sitting down to that scrumptious burger, I can attest this dairy bar is back and in good stead.

You will notice as you encounter this book for the first time, its colorful bottom outside edge. The colors denote eight regions of the state, better to assist you in deciding which culinary trip you'd like to take. Listings are more or less alphabetic in nature.

Please enjoy this effort to celebrate each and every one of the amazing dairy bars found in The Natural State, and be sure to show your appreciation to these community hubs and their staffs.

Kat Robinson
Little Rock, August 2021

Arkansas Dairy Bars:
Nostalgic and Pandemic Perfect

Today I'd like to talk about a sector of our culinary industry that is the perfect business model for dining establishments during a pandemic.

Ninety-four of these eateries dot the Natural State's rural landscape, and next week, Arkansas PBS will release a documentary about these short-order diners.

The subject of the film is the Arkansas dairy bar, a remnant of the time before the proliferation of franchised restaurants.

The idea for this project came to Arkansas foodie Kat Robinson in the early months of COVID-19. Kat, a 1995 broadcasting graduate of Arkansas Tech, has made her name as a food historian, author, and foodie, with some public television shows thrown in. She is a member of the Arkansas Food Hall of Fame's selection committee. She grew up eating sugar on her rice for breakfast and country-fried venison. Her books include *Another Slice of Arkansas Pie* and two volumes of *Things to Eat in Arkansas Before You Die*.

One day when Kat was hankering for an ice cream, as she says, she traveled to Malvern to see whether the dairy bar from her childhood was still in business. Mel's Dairy Bar was still standing, it looked just like she remembered, and the place was hopping. That's when she decided to write a book. In March, she and the team at Arkansas PBS began to work on the companion documentary.

The documentary, "Arkansas Dairy Bars: Neat Eats & Cool Treats," will premiere at 7 p.m. Thursday, August 19, on Arkansas PBS. This week, Arkansas PBS hosted a free advance screening at the Kenda Drive-In in Marshall.

Dairy bars evoke nostalgia for many of us who had the good fortune to live in a town with a dairy bar or whose grandparents lived near one. That was the initial appeal for Kat.

But as she traveled more than eight thousand miles to visit all ninety-four of Arkansas's diners, she realized that by their very design, dairy bars may be the perfect restaurant for a pandemic.

Think about it. A dairy bar generally doesn't have a dining room. You order your food through a window. You eat in a car or at a picnic table. Textbook social distancing.

Arkansas PBS sustained the social-distancing theme by holding its premiere of "Arkansas Dairy Bars" at a drive-in theater. The Arkansas PBS event was perfectly crafted as public family entertainment during a worldwide pandemic.

Kat is an Arkansan who understands Arkansans. Like the three million other people who live here, Kat took the pandemic head-on and blazed a different route. In one of her books, she writes about the character of her state. "Arkansas is a stubborn, hang-on-by-your-teeth subsistence land that adapts to weather, new folks, and the lay of the land." That's an accurate description.

With this documentary, Kat Robinson and Arkansas PBS preserve a piece of our culinary history. They also demonstrate that with imagination, sweat of the brow, and a dash of courage, we can work our way through anything.

Governor Asa Hutchinson
Weekly radio address
August 13. 2021

River Valley

West Central Arkansas

1. Bonnie's Dairy Freeze, Fort Smith
2. Dari-Delite, Ozark
3. Dari-Delite, Paris
4. Dairy Diner, Charleston
5. Dairy Dream, Mountainburg
6. Dairy Freeze, Clarksville
7. Dee's Drive In, Coal Hill
8. Deiss' Drive In, Lamar
9. Delaware Ice Cream Shop & Deli, Delaware
10. Diamond Drive In, Clarksville
 * Ed Walker's Drive In, Fort Smith
11. Feltner's Whatta-Burger, Russellville
12. Judy's Drive In, Waldron
13. Junction Cafe, Plainview
14. Mulberry Dairy Dip, Mulberry
15. R and A's Drive In, Lavaca
16. Yellow Umbrella, Fort Smith

BONNIE'S DAIRY FREEZE

Since the 1940s, this button-order drive in has been serving up a large selection of burgers, hot dogs, and ice cream delights. The original edifice faced Midland Avenue and offered eight burgers for a dollar.

After a fire severely damaged the structure in the mid-1960s, it was torn down and a new building was constructed uphill. Herb and Doris Mays - who also owned Payless Grocery - ran the place for many years.

The Dairy Freeze has been for generations a popular place for teenagers to hang out, particularly after enjoying a movie at the nearby Skyview Drive In.

The restaurant's reputation stands on its large array of ice cream offerings and on trusty, excellent burgers of all sorts - with eleven different burgers on the menu. The deep fried burrito has long been a favorite of customers, a bean and beef burrito served with or without tomatoes, lettuce, sour cream and cheese, offered for more than 50 years now.

Dinner baskets run the gamut from shrimp to chicken to steak fingers, all served with Texas toast and gravy. Ice cream is the real star here. Dipped cones are offered in three flavors - chocolate, butterscotch and cherry. Soft serve comes in chocolate, vanilla and twist. The Peanut Cluster Parfait tops the ice cream specialties board - hot fudge and peanuts over soft serve with whipped cream, nuts and a cherry on top proves popular here. The Banana Fudge Sundae (pictured to the left) and the Strawberry Shortcake Sundae are both big sellers. Shake flavors include traditional tastes as well as cappuccino and peanut butter fudge, and any milkshake can be malted.

5400 Midland Boulevard * Fort Smith, Arkansas 72904 * *cash only*

15

DARI-DELITE of OZARK

Over the course of time, there have been two Dari-Delites in Ozark. One was of the original national chain, with the iconic vertical boards (like what you see today at Garner's Drive In in Berryville, see page 46). The other was of the early 1980s style, a dining-room style dairy bar in a low long building that was part of a regional revival. Today, Ozark's Dari-Delite is housed in a new red brick building on US Highway 64, just a few blocks off the downtown square.

The Dari-Delight still utilizes a drive-up/walk-up window and board, packed with a robust selection of local favorites, with Frito pies, egg rolls and fried fish offered alongside burgers and footlong hot dogs. There are banana splits and dip cones, and a spot-on limeade is made and sold here, a nice pairing to any afternoon repast.

402 West Commercial Street, Ozark
(479) 667-3571
Facebook.com/dariozark

16

DARI-DELITE of PARIS

The Edwards family started one of the town's largest restaurants in 1988, and despite the competition (Sonic, in this case) setting up shop next door, their Dari-Delite still brings in customers from all around the county for good, solid fare.

Any day, you can stop in for a great burger and order of fries. The restaurant has a reputation in the area for good, reasonably priced catfish dinners. On Saturday mornings, the eatery offers an Arkansas specialty, chocolate gravy poured over fresh baked biscuits. There's also a full breakfast menu, and the parfaits are excellent.

An often overlooked standout is the Dari-Delite's beans and cornbread. These pinto beans are started the night before and continue to happily bubble away all day until you order them - which means, if they're still available in the evening, they're at the peak of savory creaminess. Enjoy with that slightly sweet corn muffin.

1315 East Walnut Street, Paris * (479) 963-6011

Facebook.com/DariDelitParisAr

17

DAIRY DINER

The iconic whitewashed edifice catty-corner from the local high school was originally opened in 1961 as a simple stand-alone dairy bar with a dining room on one side, and in the 1980s, a big game room was added to the other.

Shelly Stubblefield began working at the Dairy Diner when she was 14 years old. When the owners decided to close in 2017, she stepped up and took over, buying the place. "We can't close it up," she says. "It means too much to the community.

The menu of traditional dairy bar fare is highlighted by a chocolate malt that is perhaps the maltiest malt that's ever been malted, a veritable Whopper of a milkshake confection. Burgers, hot dogs, chicken sandwiches and onion rings are all a good bet.

420 East Main Street, Charleston * (479) 965-2254

DAIRY DREAM

Robert Willroth opened the two window Dari-Delight style operation in 1954. He passed it on to his son Jerry, and the family still runs it today.

The Mountainburger is one of only two loose-meat burgers you can find in Arkansas (the other being a hot dog borne version at The Original Scoop Dog in North Little Rock, see page 214). The ground beef concoction is similar to a Sloppy Joe, with more meat and less sauce, served with mustard, pickle, onion and a slice of cheese.

The Dairy Dream also sells homestyle burgers, corn dogs, Frito chili pies and all that, but it's best known as a place to get a cold treat. On a hot summer day, that choice is an ice cream cone, and rather than just stick with tiny cones and squirts of soft-serve, Dairy Dream offers three cone sizes (the large cone is to the right here). There are sundaes and freezes, malts and shakes, and drinks include Purple Cows, Silver Saddles and Baby Elephants. The Dairy Dream is open seasonally, usually May to October.

1600 US Highway 71B NE, Mountainburg * (479) 369-2295

20

21

DAIRY FREEZE

There have been several dairy bars that have graced Johnson County over the years, like the former Tastee-Freeze, the old Dairy King and the still-in-business Diamond Drive-In across the street (read more on page 26). Clarksville Dairy Freeze operates out of a 1980s era building, with such specialties as chicken gizzards, fried okra and a pizza steak burger alongside the classics. There's a ridiculous number of housemade fried pies offered, including the unusual butterscotch and vanilla varieties. The soft serve ice cream comes in cones (dipped, twists, flavor-burst are options) and in delicacies ranging from a sail-boat (a banana split without the banana)) to par-faits to this scrumptious rocky road sundae, a concoction of toasted coconut, marsh-mallow cream, pecans and soft serve chocolate ice cream.

1201 West Main Street, Clarksville * (479) 754-8009

HONORABLE MENTION - ED WALKER'S DRIVE IN

While there's no external walk-up window at the oldest continually operating restaurant in Fort Smith, Ed Walker's is tied to the many traditions of our dairy bars - great burgers, rich and creamy shakes, and a place to dine in your car. The Towson Avenue favorite, open since 1943, has pull-up service. Flash your lights for a carhop, or place your order by phone. It's also the only place in Arkansas where you can have beer delivered to your car.

1500 Towson Avenue * (479) 783-3352 * *edwalkersdrivein.org*

23

1979

DEE'S DRIVE IN

Dee and Tyke Yates opened the original Dee's in a 20x20'
building with no dining room and a window for service in
1968. The original building burned in 1972. Two years later,
the couple opened the current location, with a larger kitch-
en, a
large dining room with fireplace on one side and a large game room with a
pool table on the other. Dee cooked, Tyke served beverages and the restaurant became the hub of the community of Coal Hill.

Today, the longstanding drive in still serves its incredibly diverse menu
in all its glory, from pizza burgers to pork tenderloins, breakfast to
tater babies. The star, though, is the Leroy Burger, a remarkable
four-patty concoction where American
cheese is placed in-between each
of those firmly smashed hamburger rounds for a meaty,
cheesy, addictive sandwich
unlike any other.

306 East US Highway
64, Coal Hill
(479) 497-1777

DEISS' DRIVE IN

A walk-up window, a drive-thru window, and a dining area - means this community eatery taps all the bases when it comes to dining needs. The shakes are smooth and come in vanilla, chocolate, strawberry and pineapple. The Hickory Burger is a standout, with just the right amount of smoke imparted on the bun. A good standby for a midday meal on this friendly stretch of US Highway 64.

350 West Main Street, Lamar
(479) 885-2442
Facebook.com/DeissDriveIn

25

DELAWARE ICE CREAM SHOP AND DELI

One of the newest dairy bars in Arkansas, this adorable red-white-and-blue stand close to Lake Dardanelle is the perfect spot to grab a bite and a treat before or after a day on the lake. While the lobby has recently re-opened, you can still order through the window or online if you'd like to stay outside.

The menu is thick with a selection of pizzas, deli-style sandwiches, burgers and baskets. Sandwiches like the toasted turkey sandwich come dressed to suit, with ample amounts of meat and cheese, vegetables and condiments of your choice. You can get them on white bread, wheat bread or a hoagie roll - the latter of which is excellent for sharing.

The ice cream here is scooped instead of soft serve, with plenty of outrageous flavors like spumoni, cotton candy, salted caramel and huckleberry. Shakes, malts, and banana splits are all customizable, and you can get a scoop or two in a housemade waffle cone for an extra special treat.

26168 East Arkansas Highway 22, Delaware
(479) 234-4555
DelawareDeli.com

26

27

DIAMOND DRIVE IN

Selling signature burgers and shakes since 1967, Diamond Drive In offers more menu items to satisfy any taste, from chili dogs to catfish to broasted chicken. It's been a community favorite that's changed little since it first opened.

The shrimp basket has become very popular, and includes a hearty portion of shrimp, crinkle cut fries, a pair of hush puppies and an extraordinary, sweet and creamy coleslaw. It's a satisfying Friday special.

Don't skip the classic cheeseburger when you drop in. The griddle is well-seasoned and the burgers haven't changed in flavor in decades.

1206 West Main, Clarksville * (479) 754-2160
Facebook.com/DiamondDriveIn

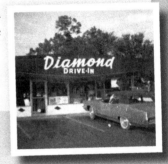

29

FELTNER'S WHATTA-BURGER

The A framed entrance to Feltner's Whatta-Burger has been traversed for decades by both Russellville residents and students at Arkansas Tech University - and it remains a stop on the pilgrimage of Arkansas Razorback fans from Little Rock to Fayetteville to boot. Come gameday, whoever's playing, the parking lot is packed both front and back.

The place was opened by Bob Feltner in 1967. His daughter, Missy Ellis, says her dad took a lawn chair out and sat by the road to count cars as they passed, to figure out the best place to set his hamburger station. The initial facility was just a walk-up dairy bar with a patio on the side, but over the years, it was expanded, and by the late 1980s the building included a huge wing with two aisles of wooden booths with yellow and green tables..

30

Mr. Feltner was well known in his community for handing out business cards. He would chat with anyone, whether they were a college freshman or a local phone lineman, people at the grocery store and families out by the park. The cards weren't just a way to get the name of his restaurant out there; they usually came with a handwritten note on the back, bearing a note, "Good for one burger," or "Good for a meal," Those cards would come back to the restaurant along with a new customer, who usually became a fan for life.

I was one of those fans. Back in my early radio days, I was procuring my once-a-week bag of fries to take back to my dorm room in Roush Hall. Mr. Feltner and I chatted while I waited for my order. He had heard about the girl who wore cat ears and played old time novelty music at the campus radio station, and he gave me a whole stack of cards to give away. It was his idea and it earned me my very first fan following, fellow hungry Tech students who loved funny songs and a really excellent meal of burger and fries.

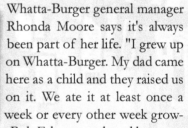

Whatta-Burger general manager Rhonda Moore says it's always been part of her life. "I grew up on Whatta-Burger. My dad came here as a child and they raised us on it. We ate it at least once a week or every other week growing up. Bob Feltner was loved by many. They say back in the day he used to keep a spoon in here. If you were a college student, he would let you write your order on that or let you charge on that spoon."

The restaurant's reputation wasn't just based on Mr. Feltner's friendliness. The burgers are just right, every time, thanks to a consistent burger assembly line that's been in place for more than 50 years. You can also get fried bologna sandwiches, grilled chicken sandwiches, grilled cheese and BLTs.

31

There is the matter of the fries. One of the reasons I'd go once a week for fries while I was in college at Tech was because a single order is a pound of fries, enough for a family, or for a college freshman to nibble on over a week. You can order yours half-size if that's too many.

Feltner's Whatta-Burger has a lot of fans - but none quite like Chris Costlow. Kelly Lilley, one of the restaurants many employees, told me about this guy. "So we have this amazing customer named Chris. He comes to us virtually every day, If he does not show up in the morning, we know something's amiss. So we will look for him:

"A lot of times we will have a bag ready to go for him, because we know he's going to get a regular burger plain with his half French fry, extra crispy, and we get it on the grill as soon as we see him pull in," she says. "He is our best customer, hands down."

"I don't deviate at all," Chris shares. "If I ever did, they might have a heart attack!"

I managed to catch him on one of his daily runs.

"I have always been a burger and fry eater, since I was a little kid," he continues. "When I moved here in 1993, I saw this place. I was familiar with the other Whataburger, that's a different corporation, when I lived in Texas. I thought, 'that's strange,' but boy, these burgers are a lot better, and a lot bigger, and the fries are huge. and I was like 'so these blow that one away,' so I was hooked."

I asked him how many Whatta-Burgers he thought he'd eaten over the years.

"I guarantee, it's probably approaching ten thousand. I'd have to do the math, but ten a week, 530 a year... maybe twenty thousand. They know exactly what I want. They treat me like gold."

Feltner's Whatta-Burger is that sort of place. Everyone's treated marvelously, and the food is steady and good. The shakes come in so many flavors, from pineapple to peanut butter, and they're nice and thick. Many dip their fries in their shakes.

For a couple of decades, the restaurant would be shut down the two weeks before classes began at Tech, for a thorough deep cleaning and a change in the decor. Over the years, Mr. Feltner would show off his collection of kites, different cartoon memorabilia, those sweet and silly puns and quotations carved into wooden plaques, and dozens of Best of Arkansas awards dating back decades from the Arkansas Times. Recently, a new honor went up on the wall - a Great State of the Plate, noting Feltner's Whatta-Burger as a member of the Arkansas Food Hall of Fame. It joins pieces of memorabilia that the employees asked to be brought back to the walls.

The restaurant that Bob Feltner decided to locate in what was essentially a pasture back in 1967, is now located right next to Arkansas Avenue and the main entrance for Arkansas Tech University. I expect it'll be there another 50 years from now.

1401 North Arkansas Avenue, Russellville * (479) 968-1401
Whatta-Burger.com

33

JUDY'S DRIVE IN

Ice cream? Judy's has it. Burgers? Those too. Big plate lunches, Ark-Mex foods and fried pies? You can get any of these delights on the old highway north of downtown Waldron. The local favorite may not be world-famous, but it's a perfect spot for an afternoon repast, with a pond out back and plenty of seating both indoors and out.

Of note is the Bru Burger, a gigantic two-patty monstrosity with American and Swiss cheeses, mushrooms and bacon, grilled onions, tomatoes, lettuce and pickle. Enough for two people, or one very, very hungry dairy bar lover.

1024 North Main Street, Waldron * (479) 637-0803
Facebook.com/JudysDriveIn

34

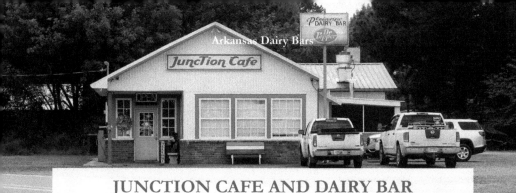

JUNCTION CAFE AND DAIRY BAR

This longtime River Valley mainstay may be way off the beaten path, but it manages to hang on and survive. Recent new owners have added to the traditional diner and dairy bar menu, augmenting breakfasts and burgers in a Cajun style. In addition to traditional omelets and French toast, there's now shrimp and grits and Cajun sausage. Burgers are available in traditional, Razorback and Ragin' Cajun styles. And there's crawfish Etouffee, gumbo and boudin alongside fish, hamburger steak and shrimp dinners. Get your ice cream in a cone or shake, or go for a slice of pie or even a pair of fluffy beignets with your choice of sauce. Pickup window is around the back.

808 West Arkansas Highway 28, Plainview * (479) 272-2450

35

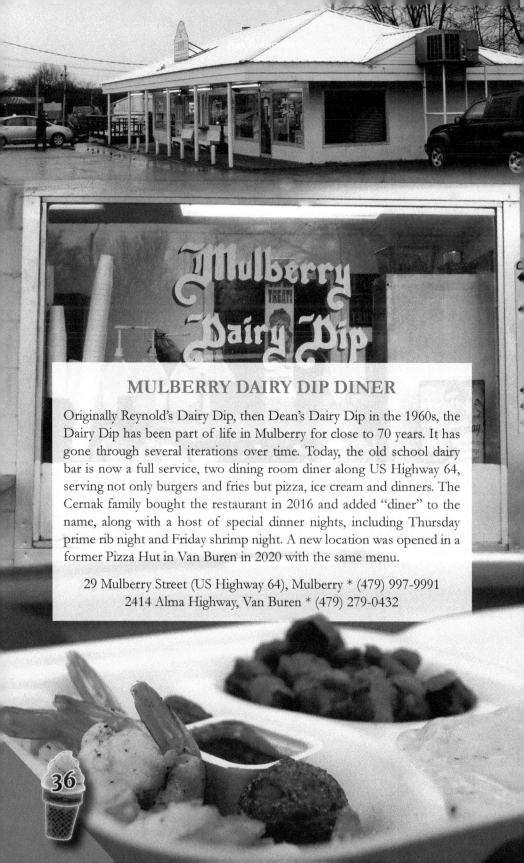

MULBERRY DAIRY DIP DINER

Originally Reynold's Dairy Dip, then Dean's Dairy Dip in the 1960s, the Dairy Dip has been part of life in Mulberry for close to 70 years. It has gone through several iterations over time. Today, the old school dairy bar is now a full service, two dining room diner along US Highway 64, serving not only burgers and fries but pizza, ice cream and dinners. The Cernak family bought the restaurant in 2016 and added "diner" to the name, along with a host of special dinner nights, including Thursday prime rib night and Friday shrimp night. A new location was opened in a former Pizza Hut in Van Buren in 2020 with the same menu.

29 Mulberry Street (US Highway 64), Mulberry * (479) 997-9991
2414 Alma Highway, Van Buren * (479) 279-0432

36

R & A'S DRIVE IN

Originally opened in 2005 and reopened in 2018, this tiny dairy bar boasts both a drive thru and walk-up window, with plenty of items to select. There are a fine selection of Angus beef burgers, including one touted on social media as the Nathan Burger - a tall sandwich featuring four big beef patties and four slices of cheese. Banana splits and soft serve cones are good bets here, as is this excellent taco burger, a loose taco meat burger with cheese, lettuce and salsa. Be sure to drop in during Girl Scout cookie season for limited time Samoas and Thin Mint shakes.

702 West Main Street, Lavaca * (479) 674-0070

37

THE YELLOW UMBRELLA

Just up Greenwood from Ballman Elementary is this tiny but distinctive structure that offers burgers, ice cream and snow cones during the week. The Yellow Umbrella has changed little since its opening in 1957, when James Beasley built the stand right next to his small store, naming it the Tastee-Freez Drive In. In 1961, it was purchased by the owner of the nearby Sunnymeade Drive In, Leo Byrum, who renamed this spot Byrum's Tastee-Freez. Along the way, it's had a lot of names, but today it still bears the distinctive circular Tastee-Freez arc above, now protected by another aluminum pavilion top over it all.

The burger shack became well known for small, inexpensive burgers, good lemonade and a double ice cream cone that had two sides for two scoops. Today, the ice cream is soft-serve, in vanilla, chocolate, and twist. The burgers are still smashed on the grill. Hot dogs, chili dogs, corn dogs and nachos are all available, as are sundaes, shakes and sno-cones. But they're only available between 10:30am and 4:15, Monday through Friday. The stand just started to recently take credit and debit cards.

1608 Greenwood Avenue, Fort Smith * (479) 783-7929
Facebook.com/YellowUmbrellaFortSmith

39

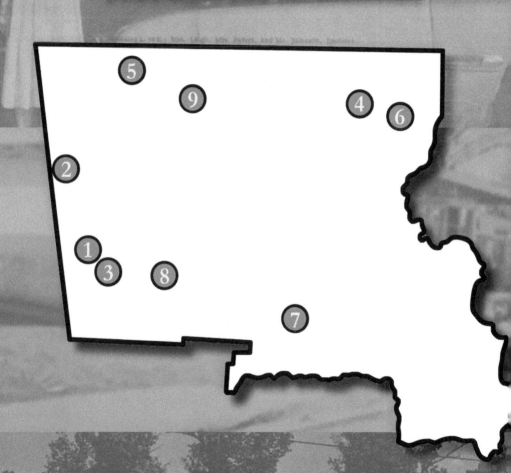

Western Ozarks
Northwest Arkansas

1. **American Drive In, Lincoln**
2. **Barnett's Dairyette, Siloam Springs**
3. **BurgerLand, Lincoln**
4. **Garner's Drive In, Berryville**
5. **Hiwasse Hilton, Hiwasse**
6. **Jim's Drive In, Green Forest**
7. **Saints Snack Shack, Saint Paul**
8. **Sugar Shack, West Fork**
9. **Susie Q Malt Shop, Rogers**

AMERICAN DRIVE IN

Since 1958, this tilt-window stone-clad dairy bar has served the far western city of Lincoln with very few changes overall. The same colors, the same window service, the same awning style and even the same name have endured over the years.

The menu features burgers, hot dogs and even a "chickie dog," where the wiener is replaced with a fried chicken strip. The restaurant is also known for its dinners, whch cover everything from shrimp to chicken gizzards, all served with French fries, coleslaw and a slice of Texas toast.

The restaurant prides itself on marvelous hot fudge sundaes of various sizes. Its dipped cones are larger than most, served with a thick layer of the chocolate shell.

303 West Pridemore Drive, Lincoln * (479) 824-5459

BARNETT'S DAIRYETTE

Ervie Barnett opened this old fashioned neon-clad dairy bar in 1957. The family owned the operation until 2017, when it was sold to local resident Jason Freese, who continues many of the traditions today.

While the original shop sold doughnuts in the morning, this later day version has expanded to full-scale dining and goes all-in on hamburgers, different types of fries, hot dogs and a variety of ice cream confections, like the whipped cream decked delicacy of a thick brownie topped with ice cream and hot fudge sauce.

Barnett's also offers a dozen different regular shake favorites, along with specials such as the lemon cookie shake with huge chunks of lemon sandwich cookies rolled into the rich and creamy soft serve. Malts are also available.

111 West Tulsa Street, Siloam Springs
(479) 524-3211
Barnetts.com

44

BURGERLAND

Originally opened in 1983, this family restaurant isn't just a burger joint - though you can be excused for thinking so, considering the name. The menu features chicken strips and nuggets, a selection of deli sandwiches including a Reuben sandwich, pastrami, and a couple of variations on the Philly cheesesteak. Sides cover the gamut from French fries to fried zucchini, and in addition to floats and shakes, you can get a big scoop of hot cobbler topped with ice cream as well.

That being said, there's a reason BurgerLand has its name. It comes down to the marvelously simple yet tasty hand-patted burger patties on its no-nonsense burgers,, griddle-fried to order and served at the long bar that dominates the restaurant or out the walk-up or call-in window, that keep bringing people back through the door.

802 East Pridemore Drive, Lincoln * (479) 824-3724
Facebook.com/LincolnBurgerLand

There are hundreds of tiny dairy bars all over the United States built in the Dari-Delite model - two-window boxes in a kit-style concrete block building with a rectangular fin on top. These would bear the words Dari-Delite on their face, sometimes prefaced with the name of the business owner or the local town.

While two Arkansas restaurants still go by the Dari-Delite name (Dari-Delite in Ozark and Paris), most of these small ice cream shacks have been bought and re-named or transformed into other businesses over the years.

The charm of the architecture was the ability to create these structures wherever they were needed. They usually consisted of a single large kitchen room, with a counter up front to take orders, a grill at the back to cook burgers, and a table in-between to create dairy desserts. Some included an outdoor entrance restroom or two on the back, or an awning for cars on the front.

47

GARNER'S DRIVE IN

The original flat-top Dari Delite opened in 1957 looks a little different now, with a later-added peaked roof and a paint job, but it's still the place to stop when you get to Berryville if you'd like any sort of ice cream confection or dairy bar fare. The menu is incredibly extensive, with not only burgers and hot dogs, fries and chicken sandwiches, but unusual concoctions such as Irish Fries and The Bomb (French fries topped with BBQ beef, cheddar cheese, ranch dressing and bacon). Most any vegetable is available fried (okra, cauliflower, green beans, mushrooms, pickles).

The ice cream delights are numerous, not only a large variety of shakes but the Strawberry Twinkie in Paradise (like a strawberry shortcake, but with a Twinkie), the Chocolate Chip Cookie Extreme, the popular Tropical Island Dream shake, Oreo Hot Fudge Bliss, and the Banana Express - a shake of bananas and vanilla wafers.

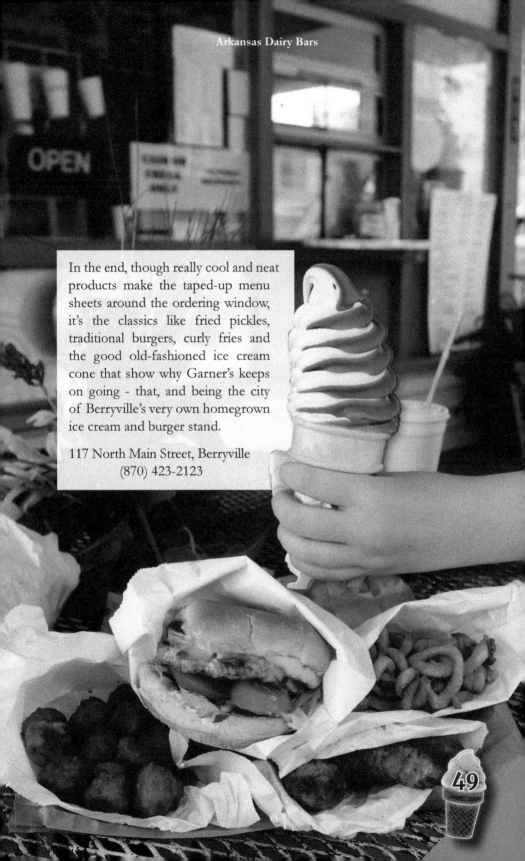

In the end, though really cool and neat products make the taped-up menu sheets around the ordering window, it's the classics like fried pickles, traditional burgers, curly fries and the good old-fashioned ice cream cone that show why Garner's keeps on going - that, and being the city of Berryville's very own homegrown ice cream and burger stand.

117 North Main Street, Berryville
(870) 423-2123

49

HIWASSE HILTON

Opened in the early 1960s as Ken's Hiwasse Dairy Freeze, the restaurant's staff answer to many names, including Hiwasse Diner like the sign says out front. But that same staff answers the phone "Hiwasse Hilton!" and it has stuck.

You won't find big write-ups about this place, which has been added onto several times over the years. The folks who visit are regulars - retirees who live in nearby Bella Vista, families from Gravette, and area vacationers who have returned repeatedly over the decades. They come for ample breakfasts, comforting plate lunches, the occasional burger and wedge of pie. But on Saturday night, they come for the prime rib, which you can order at the window to enjoy at home or on the dash of your car, a fork-tender prime rib cooked to order, salad, baked potato, green beans and a hunk of Texas toast. Be prepared to wait - it's worth it.

13548 West Highway 72, Hiwasse * (479) 787-6809

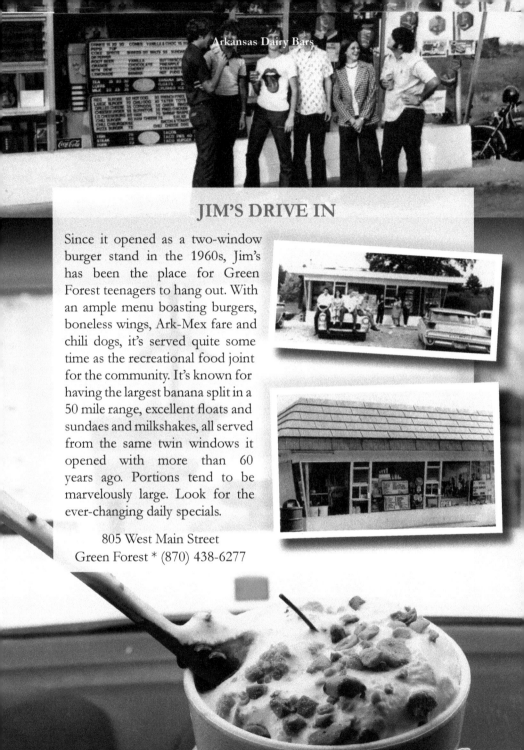

JIM'S DRIVE IN

Since it opened as a two-window burger stand in the 1960s, Jim's has been the place for Green Forest teenagers to hang out. With an ample menu boasting burgers, boneless wings, Ark-Mex fare and chili dogs, it's served quite some time as the recreational food joint for the community. It's known for having the largest banana split in a 50 mile range, excellent floats and sundaes and milkshakes, all served from the same twin windows it opened with more than 60 years ago. Portions tend to be marvelously large. Look for the ever-changing daily specials.

805 West Main Street
Green Forest * (870) 438-6277

51

SAINTS SNACK SHACK

A perfect dish for motorcyclists, off-roaders and others who find the Pig Trail a magnificent stretch of asphalt, this triple-toast onion ring and barbecue sauce double cheeseburger comes with grilled onions, bacon and whatever else you may like, made to order by a lovely woman who'll also take your order on the front porch of this humble eatery.

480 Madison Avenue, Saint Paul * (479) 677-3023

52

SUGAR SHACK

Uncle and nephew team Jerry Don and Brandon Spurlock opened this 21st century dairy bar by the railroad tracks in downtown West Fork in 2017. The restaurant's reputation was quickly cemented with its nicely seasoned, hand-patted burgers and scoop ice cream shakes. There is a drive up window in the back if you'd like to stay in the car; when orders are slow, the crew delivers right to your car. Be prepared to wait a little bit, since absolutely everything is cooked to order.

280 West Main Street, West Fork * (479) 502-1004
Facebook.com/SugarShackWestFork

53

SUSIE Q MALT SHOP

The iconic Susie Q Malt Shop has stood just outside Rogers' downtown for almost 61 years. Its name, however, doesn't come from a popular Credence Clearwater Revival song.

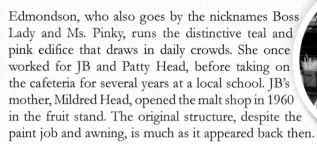

For real appetite appeal Suzi-Q'd Idahos French fried to a golden brown can't be beat.

"Back in the day, they used to have a French fry cutter and it was called Susie Q. And when you would put your potato in there, it would do the curlicue fries" says manager Sheila Edmondson. "And when I came back to take it over, the machine was gone. But we still have Susie Q fries."

Edmondson, who also goes by the nicknames Boss Lady and Ms. Pinky, runs the distinctive teal and pink edifice that draws in daily crowds. She once worked for JB and Patty Head, before taking on the cafeteria for several years at a local school. JB's mother, Mildred Head, opened the malt shop in 1960 in the fruit stand. The original structure, despite the paint job and awning, is much as it appeared back then.

The chipper Ms. Pinky didn't stay away too long.

"I stopped in here 13 years ago and asked if I could buy the grill so I could open up a restaurant at Rocky Branch Marina. Instead they offered me the Susie Q. and I've been here for 13 years."

Edmondson and I conducted our lively conversation one Thursday morning, as customers called in and came to the window, and her never-slacking staff continued to flip burgers, make milkshakes, dollop chili onto footlongs and pulled fountain drinks.

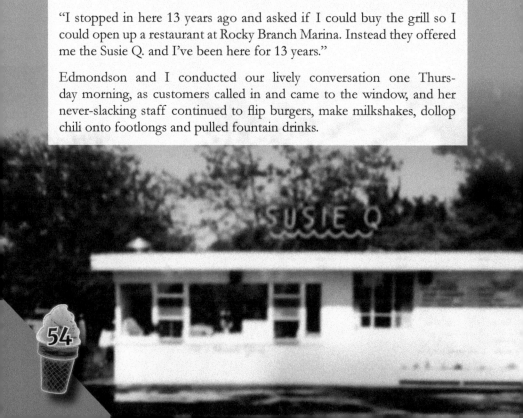

Many of those cups bear messages to particular customers.

"We take care of our veterans and our police department, our EMTs, our ambulance, our fire department. We write them a note on their cups that says thank you for your service, or it just says thank you, because some of our vets don't like to be reminded that they have bad memories, so, we just give them a little note that says thank you for everything, and they always seem to tag the Susie Q in it and say thanks, you made my day."

Everyone gets a smile on their cup. That attitude is very on-brand for the Susie Q, where the ladies behind the glass are always upbeat and bright, sporting tie dye shirts and often dancing along to the soundtrack of music that smoothly drifts from speakers both within and without the building.

"The Susie Q gives me energy. it's all due to this place. It's kinda like an energized place to work at. Can't be slow. It's fast paced," Edmondson shares as she passes a footlong from the grill station across to one of the other ladies, who ladles on chili before passing to a third woman who shakes cheese and onions onto the dogs. That footlong wiener was first cooked in the deep fryer before being finished on the grill and slid into a mustard-toasted bun.

The mustard is part of the particular flavor a Susie Q burger, dog or sandwich brings to the table… or dashboard.

"It just gives it that flavor, and it's really good," says Edmondson. "You take the bottom of your bun and you put mustard on it, and we toast it into the bun, and then you put your pickles, onions, lettuce, tomato on it. I always tell (customers), if you don't like mustard, at least try it. If you don't like it, bring it back and I'll buy you another one. Because you can't taste the mustard, it's toasted in there really good."

The patties are excellent as well.

"Hamburger patties are weighed in the back and pressed with patty papers in between them. And they're stacked, and the grill girl gets to pull them out. So they're already round, so we just put them on the grill and put our special seasoning on them."

"Do you use any special seasoning?" I ask amid the growing bustle of lunchtime.

"Yes we do!" she replies.

"And are you going to share with me what's in that seasoning" I try.

"No, I cannot - that's a secret recipe!" Edmondson laughs."

Each day, some 60-80 pounds of hamburger is patted out for burgers. During the height of summer, that amount increases to 120 pounds - making it one of the busiest burger joints in the region.

The flavors of other Susie Q creations, recipes held over from the Head family days, also define the place, like the coleslaw and the potato salad. Edmondson herself flattens and hand-breads the chicken breasts served in the baskets and on some of the sandwiches.

"That's the Cocka-Doodle Piggie! It's a big chicken breast with a quarter pound of shaved ham!" she proclaims, as one is assembled on the grill. It's a massive sandwich, probably more than a pound total. She points out a big burger being assembled. "The Big Daddy is a double cheeseburger with a quarter pound shaved ham and bacon, three pieces of cheese. That's the Big Daddy."

In addition to the new sandwiches, Edmondson has added portabella mushrooms, sweet corn nuggets, cheese sticks, and fried cheesecake. But all the original menu items are still there.

Those shakes, though…

"The shakes are really thick," Edmondson shares as she offers a large-bore straw to a customer from a bag to use in his dessert. "We can make you a 50 mile shake. I made a shake the other day for some customers that live in Grove, Oklahoma, for lunch. Their shake made it all the way back to Grove. It was still thick. We can tip a shake upside down ... It's like a concrete, but it's homemade ice cream."

Customers come back for those beloved fries, burgers, and shakes. They also come for the nostalgia - and for the special way every diner is treated.

"They have a lucky number. Everybody gets a lucky number, and we call out the lucky number and say, we hit the microphone and say lucky number so and so your order is ready. And if they have a call-in, this is a put out window. so they come up here and get their food, too."

"And why is that so lucky?" I ask.

"Because they're eating here and everyone has to get lucky every once in a while!" she replies.

Edmondson notes the shop would be nothing without her excellent employees, who work together smoothly in the rather tight environs of the small building. But most of all, she thanks the folks who come back, time after time, to enjoy the repasts offered through the window.

"If it wasn't for the customers, we wouldn't be here. So we have to treat our customers with the utmost respect."

612 North Second Street, Rogers
(479) 631-6258

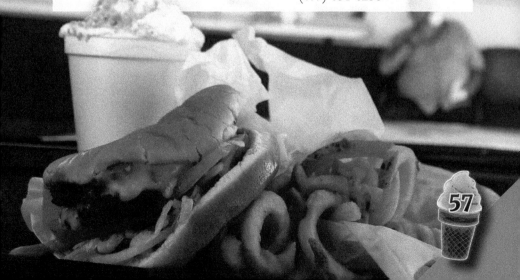

57

Eastern Ozarks

North Central Arkansas

1. American Burger Center, Melbourne
2. Bigger Burger Better BBQ, Batesville
3. Brad & Dad's Drive In, Timbo
4. Carolyn's Razorback Ribs, Yellville
5. Daisy Queen, Marshall
6. Daisy Queen Hi-Boy, Harrison
7. Frank's Hickory House, Choctaw
* Kenda Drive In, Marshall
8. Krispy House, Mountain View
9. Moore's Dairy Creme, Newark
10. Neighborhood Diner, Harrison
11. Pleasant Plains Dairy Bar, Pleasant Plains
12. Taylor's Freez King, Gassville
13. Top Rock Drive In, Alpena

AMERICAN BURGER CENTER

There's a reason burgers are in the name of the business here - with a large selection of prime hand-patted burgers on the menu, you absolutely cannot go wrong here. Of note is the Prescott Burger, with its gorgeously caramelized onions and mushrooms, perfectly toasted bun and condiments, there's little you won't love about this creations. Soft-serve ice cream, cakes, pies, and plate lunches are also superb.

1215 East Main Street, Melbourne * (870) 368-4338

BIGGER BURGER BETTER BBQ

The former E&B Bigger Burger was well known for its larger-than-normal hand-patted burgers. It was begun by EJ Biggers (hence Bigger Burger) and became a Batesville mainstay. Since November 2019, the Walls Family has taken the longtime establishment and redefined it by adding smoked pork butt, brisket, ribs and wings to the menu. The result? A marvelous dairy bar re-imagined in a way that enhances the original concept. Fortunately, those hand-patted burgers are still available, as are thick shakes and fried pies. Be sure to try the smoked chicken sandwich, and don't miss the incredible brisket and cheese stuffed bacon wrapped jalapeños known as Razorback Poppers.

1270 North Central Avenue, Batesville * (870) 569-4097

Kat Robinson

BRAD N DAD'S DRIVE IN

After the closing of the Timbo Dairy Bar in 2020, this crossroads dairy bar came back through cousins of the original owner, returning the location to its original name. These excellent burgers come on toasted seedless buns. Lots of side items to choose from, including a hand-breaded onion blossom best shared with others and creamy soft-serve. Try the brownie fudge sundae for a delectable treat after a float or hike.

6986 Arkansas Highway 66, Timbo
(870) 746-4733 * Facebook.com/BradNDadsDriveIn

CAROLYN's RAZORBACK RIBS

Housed in a former Dairy Queen on the east side of Yellville, this dairy bar offers hand scooped flavors alongside a massive Texas barbecue menu, inspired by the owners' competition-winning fare. You'll find pulled pork, ribs, brisket,chicken, and sausages all straight out of the smoker, as well as Angus beef burgers, Hog Eggs (deep fried mushrooms), and Mississippi catfish with jalapeño hush puppies. Beware the unusual, such as the Slop Bucket, which is pulled pork topped with baked beans, coleslaw and barbecue sauce - and the Tailgater Burrito, which is all of those ingredients tightly wrapped in a tortilla. The easy pick is the Cave Man Meal, which is simply a half pound each of brisket and chicken, plus four ribs.
Ice cream flavors vary, though chocolate and vanilla are always available. Cherries Jubilee is rather nice.

369 US Highway 62 East, Yellville * (870) 449-7427
1517 North Main Street, Harrison * (870) 741-7427

Kat Robinson

DAISY QUEEN

Serving Burgers with Taste Since 1966

O UR BURGERS ARE
CERTIFI ED ANGUS
NOTHING BUT THE BFST

64

DAISY QUEEN

One of the most well-known dairy bars in Arkansas has served hungry travelers and locals for more than 50 years. The Daisy Queen, owned and operated by Jeff and Robin Mays, is likely the most popular place to stop in all of Searcy County.

The eatery has sat along US Highway 65 since 1966. Jeff took over managing the restaurant from his parents, Bill and Patsy Mays, in 1989, and bought it outright in 2002; The original structure was located a short distance away and was built in 1960.

"I was three months old when they took this and bought it," says Jeff Mays. "It had gone through four owners, couldn't make it. So my dad went deer hunting, and while he was gone deer hunting, the owner of the Daisy Queen called my mom and said 'I'm done, I'm out of this, do you want to buy it?' and my mom said 'how much,' and told her, my dad comes back from deer hunting, and she said 'we gotta go down to the bank' and he said 'why?' and she said 'we just bought the Daisy Queen, we gotta go borrow some money.' (laughs) Dad said 'okay!'

"Mom was always the brains behind what it took. When she would buy a five pound bucket of pickles, of course, there are supposed to be so many pickles in that bucket. Well, they came out with these little half buckets of pickles, but supposed to be the same amount of pickles. She

literally counted every pickle in that smaller bucket, and when the salesman came back in, she said 'I knew there were fewer pickles in this bucket, and there are!' She's always taught me pennies make dimes, dimes make dollars, and dollars are what you take to the bank."

"My husband's father built the game room because he wanted the kids to stay off the streets," Robin shares. "His son, my husband, would run up and down the highway and so he wanted him to have a place to come on the weekend."

I've been visiting the Daisy Queen for about 40 years now, since I was a kid. One thing I've noticed is that the menu boards have multiplied.

"We operate under the philosophy that if we have a wide variety, we can hopefully feed everybody in the family that comes through that door, and everybody will be satisfied," Robin continues. "We want to offer a variety."

And there is a definitive variety of items available, from the traditional burgers and hot dogs to taco salads, fried mushrooms and unique items like the Hot Rise sandwich, a buttered and grilled Turano hoagie bun filled with sliced steak or grilled chicken.

There's a lot of variety with the burgers.

"The company I work for, they came out with this eight ounce, certified Angus beef patty, and I wanted to put it on my menu, and Robin was like 'what are you going to call it?'" Jeff tells me. "And Robin's like 'you can't use the Big Boy, all these other names that are trademarked. I can't get my mouth around it.' So I said 'I can get my mouth around it because I've got a big mouth, and hey, Jeff's Big Mouth Burger. you gotta have a big mouth to get your mouth around it,' so that's where I got that."

"For those who aren't big meat eaters, we have the four ounce Angus burger that we sell either in a hamburger or a cheeseburger, or a double or a triple," Robin elaborates. "We make those in-house every morning, they're hand-patted. We don't buy them frozen. We have short hot dogs and footlongs, get them with chili, get them with cheese, shredded or melted cheese, and also we offer coleslaw. Now our coleslaw is something we make in-house, we make that twice a week, and it's really good, it's really good."

Jeff adds, "our coleslaw recipe - it's simple. I tell people the recipe: cabbage, carrots, sugar and Miracle Whip. Not mayo - we use Miracle Whip. The key is letting it set for a day And you have to be patient and let that water separation happen and then you re-mix it up and that's what makes it so good. We do about 150-200 pounds of cabbage a week, and we sell it by the gallons and sell it by the quarts. And that's one of the things - when we have a fish fry, in the community, either to raise money or whatever the situation is, 'hey Jeff, we need some coleslaw.' And we'll fix them up. with a couple of gallons to give them. And then I sell them the fish!"

"The hush puppies are made here," Robin elaborates, "the catfish is breaded in house, the slaw is homemade and the tartar is homemade. We serve the tartar sauce in house with all our baskets, and customers request it with their French fries, they like to dip their fries in it."

Daisy Queen's tartar sauce is pink, instead of white, and quite tangy. I've seen folks put it on the hamburgers and even the hot dogs, too.

When I come, though, I enjoy my burger with chili and cheese, dig into those fried mushrooms, and dip those crinkle cut fries.

The dairy bar also offers those ice cream selections we all know and love, from banana splits to hot fudge sundaes, along with cookie sundaes, shakes and marvelous fried pies.

The restaurant shares a birth year with another iconic Arkansas treasure, the Kenda Drive-In, which you'll see on page 73.

Thing is, Jeff didn't plan to end up in the family business.

"So I went off to college. I had a job at Anheuser-Busch, being a cereal chemist with my food science degree. Me and my wife were married, and she was going to be a science teacher. So in November of 1989, my dad called me and

67

asked if I was taking the job with Anheuser-Busch. I said not yet but they told me to come find an apartment. And he said 'I'm proud of you, I think I've sold the Daisy Queen.' and I said, 'what?' and a guy had moved in here from out west and offered Dad a chunk of money. He said 'I'm gonna sell it.' And I said 'okay.' And I hung up.

"And the hair stood up on the back of my neck. And I looked at Robin, and she said 'what's wrong with you?' I said 'I want to move back to Marshall.' I told her what happened. I said 'here it is in a nutshell - I don't want to raise my family in a big city. I want to raise my family like I was raised. where everybody knows their name, where they know every back road, I don't want to raise my kids in a big city.' And she said 'well call your dad back.'

"We worked out a deal - he tried to talk me out of it, but he was proud I did. and I was proud I did. I have no regrets. I got a great college education and I'm actually using that education in my business and also in my salesman position, so I think I made all the right moves.

"This is my retirement plan. I have two girls - 26 and 21, Catherine and Sarah, and neither one of them say they're going to come back. I said the same thing, so we'll wait and see.

"I know this - as long as I'm alive, I'm going to own the Daisy Queen. I never can imagine - and I know this seems crazy - I can never imagine driving by this place and not being able to walk in the back door, make myself a double cheeseburger with mustard and onions only, a large strawberry shake, and then have to pay for it. I don't ever want to know that day."

"The same families stop by here for years and years and years, on their way to Branson or on their way to float the Buffalo or on their way back from the Buffalo," Robin shares, "and they'll tell me we've been stopping here for X amount of years, and we appreciate their business but we're part of the tourism in this county, definitely. We're a small family owned restaurant that serves American food, and we do so with great pride."

614 US Highway 65, Marshall * (870) 448-2180

DAISY QUEEN HI BOY

Originally built in the early 1960s as a part of the Fisher's Hi Boy chain, this singular Arkansas location saw business for years as a stopping-in point for people going to or coming back from Dogpatch USA, the Li'l Abner themed park designed after the famed Al Capps comic.

The signage and original plan for the restaurant was just like the Hi Boy original in Effingham, Illinois - a restaurant where you could order at a walk-up through a speaker, and where your order would be delivered via carhops in little white paper hats directly to your vehicle. By the mid-70s, the restaurant was under the name Daisy Queen.

The eatery did become a seasonal-only operation for a while after the closing of Dogpatch USA in the late 90s., but in more recent years it has returned to solid year-round availability. While the carhops are long gone, the restaurant does boast both walk-up window service and a large dining room. You can get a number of good plate lunches here, including a nice country fried steak, a veggie plate or a bowl of chicken and dumplings. Burgers are available year-round, including the original Hi Boy Hamburger from the first of the chain of restaurants..

Ice cream is still a draw. Chocolate soft-serve is available during the summer months, while vanilla soft-serve is offered year-round. The iconic sign was recently cleaned, repaired and repainted, a landmark worth a stop and a bite to eat along Arkansas Scenic Highway Seven.

8999 Arkansas Highway 7, Harrison
(870) 743-1122
Facebook.com/DaisyQueenPage

FRANK'S HICKORY HOUSE

This dairy bar began in the 1960s. In 1976, it was taken over by Frank Benedetti Jr., who with his wife Jackie, moved in a barbecue restaurant. Frank used to have a joint in Memphis called the Delta Cafe. Frank retired in 1986, selling the business to his son Joe and Joe's wife, Lora.

The spot's "Bylangwell Minu" is a menu written in Arkansaw-speak, with definitions in modern English, a throwback to a time when many of our restaurants embraced a hillbilly aesthetic.

Regardless the unusual spellings, the joint's barbecue sandwiches are unique and tasty. The barbecue pork or beef sandwiches (your choice) is thin shaved meat with a particularly piquant barbecue sauce that swamps the seedless bun, with or without coleslaw, and it's absolutely addictive. Grab it with onion rings or fries, and a chocolate or vanilla soda, a rarity at our dairy bars today that still happily satisfies.

Ice cream is always available, but beware falling into the trap of ordering the Dang Revenoor. It's a large ice cream cone, yes, but larger than you'd ever reasonably consume. Beware.

4736 US Highway 65 South, Choctaw
(501) 745-8970
Facebook.com/FranksHickoryHouseBBQ

HONORABLE MENTION - KENDA DRIVE IN

The Kenda is a drive in movie theater - and burger stand. Opened in 1966 in Marshall, just like the Daisy Queen (see page 64), the Kenda is a community institution

Kenneth and Marilyn Sanders had the Ken Theater in downtown Marshall. In 1966, they opened the Kenda Theater on the west side of town. The theater, named after their daughter Kenda is now run by Kenda and her husband Todd Dearing. It's the only year-round drive in theater left in Arkansas, with weekend only showings in winter and a Thursday-Monday schedule in the warmer months. On many Thursdays, free showings of classic movies and specials bring in locals, whether its a classic car night or just a good old-fashioned beach movie.

While the Kenda doesn't have ice cream, it does have hot grilled burgers and hot dogs, popcorn, slushes and a Searcy County original - the chocolate roll. This pastry with its cocoa filling is a specialty of the region, and Kenda's version is top quality.

107 Westwood Drive, Marshall * (870) 448-5400 * *KendaDriveIn.com*

73

KRISPY HOUSE

Originally opened in the 1940s and housed since 1985 in a hexagonal building along the main drag in Mountain View, Krispy House prides itself on not just burgers and fries but on exellent catfish, like this dinner here - crispy, generous portions served with hush puppies, crinkle cut fries and a sweet coleslaw make this a must-grab when enjoying bluegrass on the square. The marvelous funnel cakes are also not to be missed.

706 East Main Street, Mountain View
(870) 269-3144
Facebook.com/KrispyHouse101

74

MOORE'S DAIRY CREME

Originally opened in 1954, this community staple has been serving everything from family meals to milkshakes at the heart of Newark. Of note are the creamy soft serve cones and sundaes that require a detour and a sampling when you are in the region. Footlongs are ample and the chili is great.

511 Sixth Street West, Newark * (870) 799-3980
MooresDairyCreme.com

Kat Robinson

NEIGHBORHOOD DINER

The Tasty Treat, opened in the late 1950s, was converted into a combination dairy bar and diner in 1972. It maintains a splendid menu of burgers, plate lunches, breakfasts and desserts to this day. The versatility of this highway-side facility right under the ridge means you can enjoy indoor dining, picnic tables under an awning or even car dining with the greatest of ease. The bean plate's collection of fried potatoes, fried okra, beans and cornbread is a splendid reminder of Ozark native cuisine. Neighborhood diner sports an incomparable 25 different varieties of handmade fried pies, along with eight flavors of hand-scooped Arkansas original Yarnell's ice cream.

1112 North Main Street, Harrison
(870) 743-9493 * *TheNeighborhoodDiner.com*

78

PLEASANT PLAINS DAIRY BAR

Originally opened in 1966, this dairy bar recently converted its drive-up awning to an expansive deck for enjoying burgers and ice cream in the shade outside. Over the years, it opened a dining room in addition to its windows. This ridiculously tall double bacon cheeseburger between a couple of grilled cheese sandwiches is big enough to share - particularly if you are of the sort that lacks an unhinging jaw.

7649 Batesville Blvd, Pleasant Plains * (501) 345-2287
Facebook.com/tppdb

TAYLOR'S FREEZ KING

The Freez-King has served Gassville since the 1960s. In 1971, it was purchased by Wilma and Pete Taylor, new residents of the area who fell in love with the Ozarks and wanted to share their love with the folks who lived there. Their daughter Bonnie and her husband Sam took over in 1981; Bonnie and Sam's daughter Beth took it on in 2002.

The restaurant's claim to fame may be its incredible hand-pulled hand-breaded chicken strips, which are massive and served with home-made dipping sauces. There's also the substantially large and ample Panther burger, with its bacon, Swiss cheese and sautéed mushrooms - one of more than a dozen crazy and amazing specialty burgers on the menu. Add in the sundaes, floats, freezes, shakes, and malts in flavors such as Orange Dream, Snickerdoodle and Purple Cow, and a very smooth soft serve in chocolate or vanilla, and you have a perfect dairy bar meal.

208 E Main St, Gassville * (870) 435-6744
Facebook.com/TaylorsFreezKing

TOP ROCK DRIVE IN

Since the 1960s, this dairy diner has offered just about every craving Alpena can ask for - big made-to-order breakfasts with chocolate gravy as an offered side; plate lunch meat-and-threes that often include chicken pot pie and Mexican-style standards; a fine selection of pizzas; burgers and hot dogs of all sizes and a steady selection of homemade cakes and fried pies, hand-turned shakes and nifty cones. Of note - the Leopard Burger, named after the high school mascot. This pound of beef burger comes on its own special-made and toasted bun with bacon, cheese, and any toppings you want. It's more than a handful. Oh - and when you go for dessert, if you can manage it, ask for your cone to be dipped before it's filled with rich, creamy soft serve.

407 US Highway 62 West, Alpena * (870) 437-5238

Facebook.com/TopRockDriveIn

81

Upper Delta

Northeast Arkansas

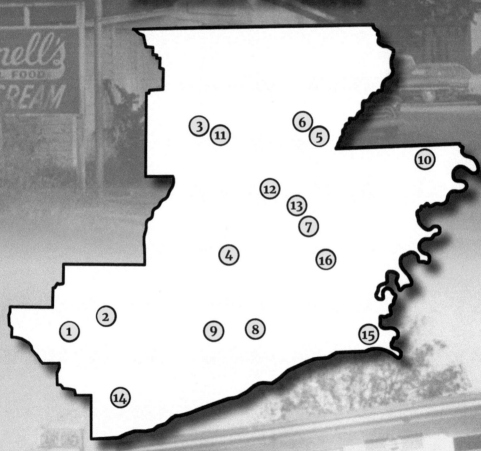

1. Barb's Bar-B-Q, Searcy
2. Bulldog Restaurant, Bald Knob
3. Dairy King, Portia
4. Dairy Shack, Waldenburg
5. Dog N' Suds, Paragould
6. Hamburger Station, Paragould
7. Hightower Dairy Freeze, Trumann
8. Johnson's Fish House, Wynne
9. Kennon's Dairy Bar, Fair Oaks
10. Kream Kastle, Blytheville
11. Polar Freeze, Walnut Ridge
12. Presley's Drive In, Jonesboro
13. Shake Shop, Bay
14. Sno-White Dairy Bar, Des Arc
15. Tacker's Shake Shack, Marion
16. Walker's Dairy Freeze, Marked Tree

84

BARB'S BAR-B-Q

Texas barbecue meets Arkansas flavor at this longtime Searcy joint. The location, formerly Pasley's Bar-B-Q, was taken over by Barbara Hill in 1984. Her family had moved from the Texas Panhandle region to Pangburn when she was in high school. The deep red barbecue sauce she uses is thick with chili and tomato flavor, and permeates the hickory-only smoked pork butts she hand-shreds..It's paired with a sweet yet stringent dijon mustard coleslaw for an extraordinarily unique flavor. Barbecue is served on seedless buns, and if you order a family pack, you'll get a bag of buns to take with you.

Burgers are also of great note here - particularly the Nacho Burger, a classic swamped with nacho cheese sauce. Barb's also offers a pork tenderloin sandwich (uncommon in Arkansas), a mean bacon chili cheeseburger, a chuckwagon sandwich, Frito chili pies and a pizza burger.

Vanilla ice cream is available in shakes, freezes, floats and scoops.

904 West Pleasure Lane, Searcy * (501) 268-3418
cash only

85

BULLDOG RESTAURANT

Bald Knob is a great crossroads in the upper Arkansas Delta. If you're crossing over on US Highways 64 or 67, going Memphis to Heber Springs, Little Rock to Jonesboro or Walnut Ridge, it's the perfect middle spot to grab a bite to eat.

Since 1978, The Bulldog Restaurant has stood at this crossroads. Originally opened by Bob and Lece Miller, today two sisters are now in charge, and they've brought their entire family into the operation. Meet Jennifer Muckelberg and Julie Roberts, the proud owners of the Bulldog.

"I was in college, and decided that I needed a part-time job, so I came to apply at the Bulldog in 1994, and been here ever since," Jennifer shares with me. "I was going to college to be a coach and a teacher, and decided that I was gonna take a year off. During that time, Bob and Lece offered me a position of assistant manager. And so I thought, 'well, I'll try that out.'"

"I started in high school, I was 15," Julie adds, "and it was when she was here. So my mom and I both came at the same time,

and been here ever since, and that's what we've been doing 20 something, 21 years. I have a daughter, she's 15 and she's working, and then I have a nine-year-old going on 18. She's the boss. I mean, she just comes in and tells everybody what to do."

"I've got a set of twins that are 17, and they're both here," Jennifer says, "and then I have a 20-year-old that's in college. Any chance she gets, she's here working."

"And then our mom, she works here also. Our dad comes in on Sundays and he fries the fish," Julie continues. "And both of our husbands, they have full-time jobs, they're a tremendous help, also."

"Then we've got some great employees that have been here, you know -"

"For a very long time. We're like a big family, you know? We're more than just, they're more than just our employees. We consider 'em family and, 'cause it's just, we're so close."

Jennifer and Julie work so closely together, they finish each other's sentences. It's evidenced in the seamless operation of the eatery, from the front counter and ice cream station to the back of the house, where on this particular day Mom is making enchiladas from scratch, the day's lunch special.

87

The Bulldog has its share of locals, but it's also the halfway point for so many people, looking for a bite to eat before or after so many activities - folks from Memphis heading to a weekend on Greer's Ferry Lake, kids going to a sports competition, travelers making a long trip from Dallas to St. Louis. The proximity of Camp Quality and Camp Takodah means it's not uncommon to see parents and children getting in a meal before or after a session. There are a lot of different reasons people stop in.

One of those reasons is a dish that's put the restaurant on the map.

"Shortcake season," Julie states.

"That starts April 1st and goes through Labor Day, 'cause everyone is anxious for that time to start," Jennifer adds. "Lucille Miller, which is Bob's mother, actually makes the shortbread at home and brings it up here. In the beginning, she would teach a few people how to make it. You know, you had to be special to learn how to make it."

I ask, "so it's a trade secret?"

"Yes, absolutely!" Jennifer laughs. "Yeah, our barbecue is a big hit, too. We're well-known for that, 'cause we have our own special sauce recipe, barbecue sauce, so it's homemade."

"Yes, and we have pork and chicken," Julie contributes. "We smoke it daily."

"And then our footlongs, everyone loves our footlongs, 'cause we have homemade chili and it's just huge," Jennifer says.

"During the fall months, we offer what's called a pecan apple cake, it's something that we just started," Julie continues. "Also, a homemade peanut butter cake we do during the fall months. During the summer, in addition to our strawberry shortcake we have our cyclones with the candy and the ice cream mixed together. We have our brownie delight, which is just out of this world, brownie, ice cream, hot fudge, what more can you say. And our ice cream, we have Flavorbursts. It's the vanilla ice cream with the strawberry or raspberry or pina colada, the flavor mixed through it that the kids just really, really love."

"Then we have our daily pies," Jennifer rolls on. "That's every day. Our coconut, chocolate, pecan, with the big homemade meringue on top of it, yes, and then we have a lemon ice box."

"And the dipped cone!" they both almost shout. Yes, the dipped cone is fantastic.

As amazing as all that is, I would be remiss if I didn't write about the burgers.

"They're fresh black Angus patties. They're never frozen." Julie says. "Cook 'em by order. They're fresh, and they come on a, you know, you can get a single burger or a double burger, and then they come with all the fixings on top. Mustard, ketchup, mayonnaise, lettuce, tomato, pickle, onion."

They're juicy, and when you get them right out of the bag as soon as you order, the bottom is so hot and the top is so cool and it's amazing.

Best thing about the Bulldog may be that it's always open at mealtime, seven days a week. The restaurant opens at eight every morning.

There's a breakfast sandwich on the menu, or you have the option of ordering a burger or anything else at all - like the plate lunches with chicken strips, steak fingers, fried shrimp. There's so many sandwiches, and salads, and of course a pizza burger.

That thick menu is much of why the restaurant maintains its clientele. There's always something someone's going to like on the menu. And it's the consistency of the products the restaurant offers - the burgers are always hot and juicy, the ice cream is always smooth, and the folks are friendly.

Like other dairy bars named after the local high school mascot, this place has managed to survive the test of time, a hub at the heart of Bald Knob, where friends and strangers both come to dine.

Jennifer and Julie both well understand the importance of the Bulldog and its ilk. They've made it a family affair.

"The Bulldog, there's not very many Bulldogs around," Jennifer shares.

"You can get your McDonald's in every town," Julie continues, "Sonics, you know, Taco Bells, but you don't get your Bulldogs in every town."

Jennifer nods. "You know, the usual customers, they always come back and make sure that they're supporting us."

3614 Arkansas Highway 367, Bald Knob * (501) 724-5195

DAIRY KING

Don't let the façade fool you - it's just a newer building for the heart of the Portia community that's been open since the 1950s. The original was a major stopping point for travelers along US Highway 63, with its classic burgers and shakes menu. It's continued non-stop ever since, and is now a plateholder for the Arkansas Food Hall of Fame.

The Dairy King has every manner of burger, hot dog and sandwich available, with weekend breakfasts, eveningtime steak dinners, and anytime catfish baskets available. And of course, there are fried pies, milkshakes and even excellent dipped cones to appreciate. Try the home-made potato chips.

205 West Front Street, Portia * (870) 886-6301

DAIRY SHACK

Absolutely perfect, crispy, crinkle cut fries have long drawn me to this establishment at the corner of US Highways 14 and 19 in Waldenburg. The D Shack, as locals call it, has been around since 1970 in this spot. Respectable, perfect hand-patted 1/3 pound dairy bar burgers are marvelous - but what die-hard locals know about are the hearty, thick cut fried bologna sandwiches dressed to order, with perfect blackened edges.

While you're there, grab a shake, a cookie, or a square of marvelous fudge if it's in the case.

796 US Highway 49, Waldenburg * (870) 579-2214

94

DOG N' SUDS

Don Hamacher and Jim Griggs opened the first Dog N Suds restaurant in Champaign, IL in 1953. The franchise grew through to the 1970s, with at one time 650 locations across the United States. Here in Arkansas, those included locations in Conway, Searcy, Jonesboro and Paragould.

Today, there are just 17 locations left across the United States. The southernmost spot is in Paragould, where you can still get your burgers, root beers and hot dogs along Kingshighway a few blocks from downtown.

What makes this location unique is Salvadorean additions to the menu - in particular, pupusas filled with beans, cheese or lorocco - any of which manage to go expertly well with the creamy, frosty root beer.

319 East Kingshighway, Paragould * (870) 236-8511

HAMBURGER STATION

In downtown Paragould, inside a Texaco station listed on the National Register of Historic Places, you'll find Bert Daggett. The self-described grease jockey and head bottle washer has been running Hamburger Station place for more than 20 years.

"I bought it in 1998 from two friends of my mom and dad who weren't ready to sell, but they were thinking about it. They came to Marianna for a golf tournament and they made some comment and I said, 'well, tell me about it..'"

The structure was purpose-built as a Texaco station in 1924. Dottie Biddick and Marky Collum started the Hamburger Station in the historic building in 1985.

"And you just thought, this is a cool idea, and you'll come up here?" I ask.

"Yeah"

"That's a little insane!"

"Yeah. You start doing it and you really like it, and there's times where you just want to throw things away and run for the hills, but somebody tells you, 'that's the best burger I've ever had!' and it doesn't matter. I keep on going.

"Dottie Biddick grew up in Oklahoma, and they were famous in some part of Oklahoma for onion burgers. She said, 'well, no one does

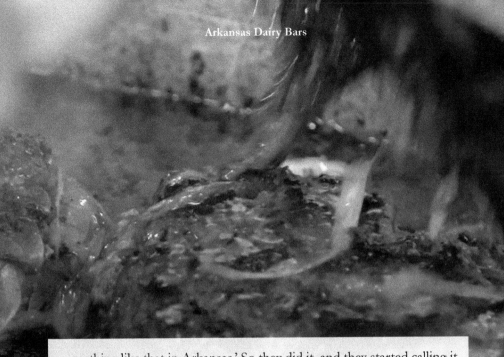

something like that in Arkansas.' So they did it, and they started calling it the Onion Burger, but then, they thought that was just not cool enough, so they said the Hum-Burger, 'cause when you're eating it, you're going, 'mmmmmmm,' you start humming!

"What sets us apart on just the burger, itself, is we do ground beef, 73/27. It's fresh and never frozen. We do patties every day. My guys come in, and they start five-ounce patties. Everything is just done on the meat, and the

only thing we put on it's salt and pepper, but when you go to the on-ions, the Hum-Burger with the onions, we do the jumbo Texas sweet onions, and we have a mandolin that shaves 'em down to where they're almost paper thin. So when you put 'em on the meat after you salt and peppered it, and they cook down and the juices go into the meat, and then, when you flip it over, you cook the onions and char 'em, and the steam from that goes up into the burger, so that they just kinda just melt into the burger. You have to toast the buns, 'cause if you put, like, a pile of hot onions and mustard and pickles on a bun, it's just gonna just melt apart."

97

The Hum-Burgers come dressed with kosher pickle chips and mustard, but you can ask for them any way you want. Lots of folks ask for the restaurant's homemade slaw, made from cabbage, Miracle Whip and a little sugar. While for decades I've had my Hum-Burger as it comes, trying it now with the slaw, I can so see it.

Bert's added a lot of variations to the menu over time, playing on the names of friends and acquaintances. A few were already listed.

"Carole is, it was already on the menu before I got it. A girl that was from here was Miss Arkansas (Carole Lawson was Miss Arkansas in 1987), and her father was a surgeon here, and so that was his favorite burger, but the ladies wanted to do something for her when she won Miss Arkansas, so they named it the Carole Burger. I was friends with Carole in college, and when she came in to eat a burger, I was like, 'hey!' and she goes, 'that's my father. I hate, hate mayonnaise!

"The Cheddy, I named that after a buddy of mine. Double meat, double cheese, and double slaw. We put on chili cheese fries with our Loaded Gasaway, we sell about maybe 10 a day."

The crowd that's formed out front are all regulars - in fact, just about everyone I meet this particular day are regulars, including the mayor. They inform me that Bert's smoked turkey isn't always available because it sells out, thanks to the thick cuts served on the turkey club and in the turkey salad.

I ask him if he changed anything when he took the restaurant over.

"No, hell no! I would get in trouble if I did that! I switched to the ranch dressing that I liked, and thought, well, heck, you know, what's the big deal? And there's a beauty shop here, Lucille's, and I got a couple phone calls one day, and they read me the Riot Act! Then I got another call from Dottie and Marky saying, 'What were you doing? We told you, don't mess with anything!'

"So I had to go back to that ranch dressing. You have a good reputation, and you don't want to mess it up, keep doing the same thing.'"

That reputation is pretty solid. Mayor Josh Agee recalls coming to the window numerous times throughout his childhood, the stand within walking distance of his home.

"When I was a kid, I would come down here and get a

cherry milkshake, fries, and the Hum-Burger, and then if I was putting a little too many pounds on, I would try to go a diet, I would eat chicken strips, 'cause I thought chicken was healthier." the mayor laughs.

Recently, Bert has found renewed vigor with tackling the day-to-day operations of Hamburger Station.

"Kim, yeah, my future wife, she's been able to step in with the helping out, and then she started just taking on little jobs and little projects. I just told her, I said, 'Hey, look, you know, it's free reign, do what you want to do.' I'm blessed to have her in my life, 'cause I didn't know how to work on Facebook or do a Facebook page, or post things. She takes pictures, and she's great at it, and I cannot express how much she's helped make me realize that I'm missing out on certain things. Like we just took cash and checks. She said, 'You'd be surprised when you take a credit card,' and I argued, but she was right and I was wrong, which I don't like to say it out loud.

"Being on that grill and everything else, when you're doing it all by yourself, it's a chore. But, yeah, I love doing the grill, that's my thing. I just love being the grease jockey. When someone sticks their head in the window and just says, 'Man, that's the greatest burger I ever had,' that puts the icing on the cake every day."

HIGHTOWER'S TASTEE FREEZE

Back in 1948, Harry Axene and Leo Moranz began developing a new type of small ice cream freezer. In 1950, they started the first Tastee-Freez in Chicago. The pair marketed the machine they created to franchisees across America, selling it at price and making money from the sale of the ice cream mix they provided. By 1953, there were more than 600 locations.

The chain grown from this start was known for selling Big T Burgers and ice cream delights. In 1982, the operation was sold to the DeNovo Corporation of Michigan. Many of the branded restaurants left the franchise but continued to operate under the name or a variation of the name for years.

The last branded Tastee-Freez location in Arkansas, Johnson's Tastee-Freez in Cabot, closed in 2019. Hightower's Tastee-Freeze in Trumann, the last Arkansas restaurant with the Tastee-Freez name (though now with an additional 'e') is independent of the chain. It offers multiple burgers, including its classic Big T. There are loads of sandwiches, and the daily special lunch plate is widely varied with anything from burnt ends to shrimp boil in the rotation. Ice cream is, of course, always in style, and you can still get a stacked parfait in a cup with whatever flavors you'd like.

149 Arkansas Highway 463 East, Trumann * (870) 483-2464

JOHNSON'S FISH HOUSE

Since 1972 with its start as the popular Johnson's Freeze Inn, this Wynne staple has always been counted on for a good meal. Over time, the menu has evolved to include not only burgers and fries but chicken fried bacon, fried green tomatoes, barbecue nachos, pulled pork sandwiches, chicken livers, ribs and frog legs.

But it's the fried catfish that has been the biggest pull, which is why this evolution of the once diminutive dairy bar is now a full-scale restaurant capable of taking in crowds for dinners. Window service is still available through the drive-thru, where you can get a classic catfish plate after a short wait, a box of fresh, hot fish, fries and hush puppies, pickle and sweet coleslaw.

Soft-serve ice cream is always on deck, particularly cones and sundaes and a nice hefty variety of shakes. The butter pecan shake is a lovely end to any meal.

329 US Highway 64 East, Wynne * (870) 238-3536
JohnsonsFishHouse.com

KENNON'S DAIRY BAR

Truly one of those amazing secret spots locals love and treasure. Hazel Kennon opened this dairy bar back in 1971. Her son Doug and his wife Judy have kept it going strong. Not much has changed since. The restaurant prides itself on a selection of Arkansas Delta dairy bar classics, including a barbecue sandwich, pizza burger, a burrito deluxe, fried bologna sandwich and of course burgers. In fact, Kennon's offers two different burgers - the regular hamburger or cheeseburger made with a four inch patty, or what's called the All-Meat Burger, a homestyle hand-patted and seasoned burger that's mighty tasty.

Kennon's offers a Hot Fudge Cake - fudge and soft-serve over fresh baked chocolate cake - and a fine selection of floats, frosted drinks, milkshakes and cones. Remember to ring the bell for service if you pull up to the drive-thru - the little dining room sometimes gets loud when busy.

131 US Highway 64, Fair Oaks
(870) 697-2009 * *cash only*

105

KREAM KASTLE

Blytheville, Arkansas, sits just below the Missouri Bootheel. Its culinary contribution to Arkansas is the pig sandwich, and it'd be hard to beat the pig sandwich at this unique dairy bar.

"In 1953, my father started out with ice cream, and then he went to hot dogs," says Suzanne Johns Wallace. "He had them six for a dollar at one time. Then he added the barbecue in 1955. That was a big hit, and it grew from there."

Suzanne is the daughter of Steven Johns, the man who first opened the Kream Kastle as a milk bar. She quite literally grew up in the restaurant.

"Oh, it was fun. You know, we got all the ice cream we wanted. My daddy would fix whatever we wanted, any way we wanted. My name's in the concrete on the, over on that side."

She and her husband, Jeff, own the business today.

"In the beginning, it was just hamburger and barbecue and French

106

MENU
Kream Kastle Drive-In
112 N. Division - Hi-Way 61
Blytheville, Arkansas

SANDWICHES

Barbecue	.35	Hot Dogs	.20
Hamburger	.30	Cheesedogs	.25
Hamburger Deluxe	.35	Chili Buns	.10
Cheeseburger	.35	ChiliBurger	.30
Cheeseburger Deluxe	.40	KastleBurger	.55
Hot Dogs	Take Home Special	6 for $1.00	
Order French Fries			.25

SHAKES 25c	MALTS 30c
STRAWBERRY	STRAWBERRY
CHOCOLATE — PINEAPPLE	CHOCOLATE — PINEAPPLE
CHERRY — BUTTERSCOTCH	CHERRY — BUTTERSCOTCH
VANILLA	VANILLA
EXTRA THICK	**EXTRA THICK**

FLOATS .20	SODAS .25
COKE — 7-Up	STRAWBERRY — CHOCOLATE
PEPSI — ORANGE	CHERRY — VANILLA
ROOT BEER — GRAPE	PINEAPPLE — BUTTERSCOTCH

Cones   5c -- 10c -- 15c

Pints	30c	—	Quarts	55c

CANDY — CHEWING GUM — CIGARETTES — POTATO CHIPS

Sundaes   --   15c & 25c

Banana Boat - 45c

fries and shakes. My father's slogan was, 'Kream Kastle, home of the Kastle Burger.' He just had a dream."

Steven Johns was the first restaurant owner in Blytheville to drop the "Whites Only" signs and fully integrate his establishment after the passage of the Civil Rights Act in 1964.

"We all need to eat, and everybody was the same to him," Suzanne affirms.

Jeff came on in the mid 1980s.

"It's been my whole life, since I was 26 years old. I'm 63 today. We got married first, and a month later, her mother put me to work," Jeff admits. "I was already working, don't get me wrong."

"I told him, I said, 'Jeff, that's a lot of hard work.' He said, 'I'm ready,' " Suzanne laughs.

Jeff kept the original dishes, but added some too. "Kastle Burger, chili cheeseburger, onion rings, French fries, steak sandwich, chicken basket, fish basket, salads, pig salads…" he rattles off.

There are also the ice cream items - all the same price, whether you get a shake, a cone, a float or a freeze.

The star of the menu, without a doubt, is the pig sandwich.

"Well, it's a pork shoulder cooked with hickory charcoal wood for 12 to 13 hours, and we chop it, or pull it, or slice it. I'll sell anywhere from 10 to 12 shoulders a day, That would be probably 200 pounds a day. A lot of work, a lot of smoke, but it takes meat, a bun, hot sauce, and slaw. And cheese, sometimes, and mayonnaise, sometimes. Chili, sometimes, and some hot sauce."

I ask what's in the sauce.

"Vinegar, pepper," Jeff begins.

"It's a secret, that's enough!" Suzanne exclaims, to which Jeff lightheartedly replies, "That's it. That's all!"

Them pig sandwiches come a standard way, unless you ask for a variance. The pit smoked pork butts are chopped fine, then placed by hand on fresh buns. Slaw and sauce are added, then the top bun is popped on and the sandwich is pressed with a hot iron to toast the bread. Some folks like chili and cheese atop the pile of pig.

"I think it's just really special for people that have grown up here eating it, and people that travel and come through, they like it, too, but it is a special sauce," Suzanne tells me. "We have many customers that will stop and buy the, you know, we bottle it now, and they will stop and take it to family elsewhere. It's really neat meeting all the people that still remember us."

Kream Kastle has a lot of regulars.

"I was born and raised here in '58, and we've been coming here forever," says John Willard, poking his head in the door while Jeff chops another round of pork. "The best barbecue in the whole tri-state area, as far as I'm concerned."

I ask him, "so what do you like on your pig sandwich?"

"Just the regular, a little bit of the slaw, and the hot sauce. You know, you can't beat it. That sauce is great. We've got a bottle at home in our refrigerator, We keep it stocked up. My kids love it. Wife loves it. I have relatives in Texas we have to send it to. I got in trouble last summer. We met my sister-in-law's family in Florida. She got mad because we didn't bring any barbecue with me!" John laughs. "If I'm not in a barbecue mood, a Kastle Burger is to die for, too.

"You know, when, back in the day, this was the little circuit... you drive around here, go back, go down to, by the high school, circle back, sometimes to stop in here and grab you a drink or a burger. It's just been a part of Blytheville forever."

"Everybody's welcome here," Jeff asserts. "They're welcome. It doesn't matter if you have any money, you can pay me the next time, or you don't pay me. I don't turn anybody away."

"When they're traveling, they'll get off at exit 63," Suzanne relates. "You know, if they grew up here, especially, and they'll have to stop here, and they'll always let Jeff know. One lady said she met her husband on one side and they got engaged on the other side."

The Kream Kastle gets its share of famous folks who poke their heads through the door, too - like weather guy and food lover Al Roker, and Governor Asa Hutchinson. Little Rock-based food and culture writer Rex Nelson introduces folks to the establishment on the regular.

The Kream Kastle used to be open seven days a week, but with changing times and grandbabies to spoil, Jeff and Suzanne have cut the hours back to weekdays only.

"You get up every morning about 6:30, and you come to work, and you stay until the day's done, whether it's at 7:00 or 10:00," Jeff tells me. "You have to have people. You can't do it by yourself."

"You just work along, do it together," Suzanne agrees. "And we love it, we do love it."

Under the broad awnings on either side,- button-press menu boards added to each stall in 1987 stand ready for those who wish to order from their vehicle.

"It's the last of the mom-and-pop eating places, that you can come and feel welcome, and everybody knows your name," Jeff shares. "If you ever walk through that door, I may not remember your name, but I know who you are, and I'm gonna make you welcome, and you don't get that. You know, that's gone by the wayside."

"I guess because it was my daddy's dream, and then Jeff's worked so hard, well, you know, we just want it to continue on," Suzanne shares.

"Blytheville's a good place to live," Jeff says. "A lot of good people here. They've all been good to me. They've helped me keep my doors open. I've made 'em welcome, they come every day, you know. We love Blytheville, and the people here."

112 North Division Street, Blytheville * (870) 762-2366

111

POLAR FREEZE

Since 1958, this barbecue dive and dairy bar has operated on Walnut Ridge's north side. That was the year Jack Allison took over the original building from its previous owner, Thurlo Davis, who let him pay for the edifice with the money he made from selling his barbecue ham sandwiches. "Pay it as you make it," Davis told him.

Allison's jukebox financed the light bill, and he managed to hang on and earn the money to outright own the Polar Freeze.. In 1968, he even managed to pay for a new building - all of $30,000 - right next door. He once recalled that he hired a group of teenagers to tear down the old place. It took less than 45 minutes.

Mr. Jack, as he was lovingly known, passed away in 2019, but not before leaving behind a 60+ year legacy of marvelous storytelling, savory sandwiches and dairy delights that still hold value in the community today.

The heart of the menu is the original barbecue sandwich, made from pork hams hickory smoked for 22 hours, served on seedless buns with a sweet sauce. That ham barbecue, rather than the pork shoulders used by most Arkansas barbecue joints, made a difference in the flavor.  Mr. Jack said Thurlo Davis taught him that, and that his eatery smoked hams instead of butts because they're less greasy.

113

Back in 2014, I sat down for a chat with Mr. Jack while working on *Classic Eateries of the Arkansas Delta*. "I bought it on first of July, 1958, and have been here on this corner all these years," he told me. "I have a manager that's been with me about 35 years, an assistant manager 25 years and when I really want to do something I just plan it and go do it!

"Walnut Ridge is a little old town. We have about 4000 population here, and everybody's been real good to me. I've had pretty good business all these years. I couldn't have had a better life. I just enjoy it mainly because I get to see all my friends. They're good friends, but they're not going to knock on your front door when you're retired. They will come by and get coffee or a milkshake and talk. If I have a day off with nothing to do I'm just bored, so… anyway...."

Mr. Jack loved to tell stories, and his most famous tale is of the night of the 18th of September, 1964, when a particular musical group had a stopover in town.

"They give me credit for it, but I really don't deserve the credit," he told me. "I was picking up paper and trash off the lot at maybe ten, eleven o'clock at night and I saw this large plane circling. We have a wonderful airport at Walnut Ridge – I thought it was unusual to see it com through the night. About that time, three teenagers came running around in a car. I asked them what they were doing and they said 'trying to run around' so I told them to go check on the airport and see what was going on with that plane, and here they went.

"An hour later they came back all excited. They said it was The Beatles. Now, I said 'don't come back into town starting some sort of rumor like that.' 'No, Jack, that's the Beatles,' they said. I didn't believe it. Because I was stationed in England for 30 months and I was 20 miles from Liverpool and that's where the Beatles started. And it was a coincidence, it really was The Beatles – so that's the story there."

Turns out, The Beatles were indeed at the airport, changing planes from Dallas, where they'd just finished a concert at Memorial Stadium, and a ranch owned by Reed Pigman in Alton, Missouri. Pigman was the owner of American Flyer Airlines; the band had chartered one of his aircraft during their tour. Their Friday night plane change that Mr. Jack saw, drew the attention. By Sunday morning, enough rumors and leads had been nailed down that a crown of 200-300 folks, mostly

teenagers, skipped church and waited at the Walnut Ridge airport. Word is, George Harrison and Paul McCartney arrived on a flight before the masses arrived, and watched from an old pickup truck. When a plane carrying John Lennon and Ringo Starr taxied in, the pair walked a gauntlet between the polite but loud fans and boarded their flight for their last concert in the United States. McCartney and Harrison joined them, ending the brief and only times The Beatles set foot in Arkansas.

"What I did, I did completely just to give those kids something to do, " Mr. Jack told me, laughing.

Though Mr. Jack has now passed, the restaurant remains robust, offering griddle-flattened burgers, thick milkshakes, a multitude of fried sides like veggie sticks and onion rings, and a picture perfect twist cone. Service is call-ahead, walk-up, dine in or drive-thru, and you can park your car right under the big shade awning on the property's triangle.

416 US Highway 67 Business, Walnut Ridge * (870) 886-9976

115

PRESLEY'S DRIVE IN

Originally opened by Hettie and Terry Presley in a former Dairy Queen along Jonesboro's Gee Street in 1977, Presley's has always been one of the coolest places in town for young folks to hang out - like these folks from Westside High... Maddona Gurley Lee, Darah Tate Watson, Angel Siebert St. Pierre, Rena Bradley Wren and Jame Beth Pierce just hanging out at Presley's, as one does.

I spent a good deal of time there myself back in the late 1990s - it was the closest restaurant to my house, and a wonderful place for breakfast or a sundae after work on the morning show at KAIT.

Today, the red-roofed Presley's Drive-In continues to offer diner-style breakfast and lunches, dipped cones, and a great patty-melt-style Reuben sandwich. Shredded corned beef set this rye bread sandwich apart from every other one I've ever had, and butter-toasting the bread just elevates it. If you go, shakes are good, but check and see what the day's pies are. Also, a nice thick selection of burgers and breakfast, too.

917 South Gee Street, Jonesboro * (870) 932-7835

116

117

SHAKE SHOP

Originally opened as Hightower's Shake Shop in 1972, then the Jeffries' Shake Shop, the Milam Shake Shop and eventually the K&C Shake Shop. this sturdy mainstay has been a favorite of Bay for generations, with fresh fruit shakes, burgers, pizza and barbecue.

Today, the must-get dish is the fish dinner offered on Friday and Saturday nights. Hot catfish, crisp fries, sweet slaw, mildly sweet hush puppies all served with an onion chunk, tartar sauce and a pickle makes for a delectable feast of perhaps the most underrated fried catfish in the state. The shakes, of course, are excellent.

205 North Bay Drive, Bay
(870) 781-3611

SNO-WHITE DAIRY BAR

Originally opened by E.L. Hinson in the 1950s, the Sno-White Dairy Freeze has served Des Arc as burger joint, ice cream stand and now family restaurant. In 2017, it reopened as the Sno-White Dairy Bar with a full-sized dining room, plate lunch specials and hand-dipped ice cream in addition to its classic soft-serve. Its banana split is legendary in both size and variety, with strawberry, cherries, pineapple, hot fudge and fresh bananas augmenting its marvelously rich ice cream.

405 Main Street, Des Arc * (870) 256-3306

119

Shake Shack
1977
THE SULTANA CHALLENGE

Kat Robinson

TACKER'S SHAKE SHACK

John and Loretta Tacker opened this dairy bar inside a former Tastee Freeze back in 1977, a place that locals say Elvis would have loved to have

visited. The little burger and pizza joint became known for being the best one-stop place to feed the family in Marion. Catfish, macaroni and cheese, plate lunches, everything the Tackers tried was quickly received and loved.

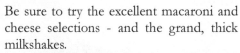

The restaurant became known for its excellent selection of pies in all sorts of varieties - cream pies, fruit pies, a marvelous hot fudge brownie pie, lattice pies, even Tang pie. Its fried pies also became noteworthy. Likewise, the massive selection of burgers have earned their own due fame, from the Italian Stallion marinara-sauced burger to the Waverly Burger's special sauce, cheese and bacon; to the epic Sultana Burger, a four-patty, chili-bacon-egg, beans and hashbrowns construction that's a hot commodity for challenge burger eaters. Consume this one, and you'll get your photo on the wall.

Be sure to try the excellent macaroni and cheese selections - and the grand, thick milkshakes.

409 East Military Road, Marion
(870) 739-3943 * *ShakeMarion.com*

121

PIZZA BURGERS

Across the state, one delicacy appears over and over again. It's so common, different restaurants brag they have the very best. However, the acclaimed pizza burger isn't an Arkansas original.

Back in 1945, Wisconsin friends Paul M. De Angelis, Sr. and Russell Hugh McGrorty decided to go into the restaurant business. Their Muskego Drive In became very popular at a time when drive ins and dairy bars were taking over the landscape. The two were looking for an item that would make their eatery distinctive. De Angelis came up with an idea - a play on steak sandwiches that would have the flavor of a fresh baked pizza. Over several weeks, he researched the idea, eventually perfecting a blend of spices, herbs and meat to create the breaded patty known today as the pizza burger.

The drive in flourished; the partners sold tons of pizza burgers, and in 1953 they started marketing their products worldwide. Today, these flavorful breaded patties are sold nationwide through Pizza-Burger System Incorporated.

I have found pizza burgers throughout the state, in at least two thirds of all the dairy bars represented in this book. But I also noticed that the delicacy all but disappeared several months into the pandemic, as manufacturing delays and work stoppages caused a pizza burger gap. Fortunately, supply chains are back up and pizza burgers are once again available all over the state.

Most pizza burgers are dressed with lettuce, tomato and mayo by our dairy bars. A few add marinara or do a full-out hamburger LTOP dressing on the sandwiches. Whatever way you like them, pizza burgers are almost certainly here to stay.

WALKER'S DAIRY FREEZE

Originally opened in 1951, this two-window wonder has stood the test of time, offering fries, snow cones and pizza burgers to generations of local families. That pizza burger is a star - expertly fried and served with lettuce, tomato and mayo, it's a memory right out of time, served on a toasted bun. Consider a Tiger's Blood snow cone or a vanilla shake when you stop in.

101 US Highway 63 West, Marked Tree * (870) 358-2508

123

Lower Delta

Southeast Arkansas

1. **Burger Shack, Helena West Helena**
2. **Hornet's Nest, Hazen**
3. **Hughes Drive In, Hughes**
4. **Lion's Den, Clarendon**
5. **Pic-Nic-Ker Drive In, Dumas**
6. **Rich's Hamburgers, Pine Bluff**
7. **Troy's Drive In, DeWitt**
8. **White River Dairy Bar, DeValls Bluff**
9. **Willy's Old Fashioned Hamburgers, Dermott**

BURGER SHACK

You wouldn't need to be the only person to think this place is called Best Coke in Town, thanks to the big bold signs on either side of this classic dairy bar which has been a local favorite for more than 50 years.. And the Coke, somehow or another, really does shine here. But it's not the only reason to drop by. The extensive menu includes a selection of breakfast biscuit sandwiches, po'boy sandwiches and two sets of burgers - the All Beef hamburger and cheeseburger, which are 1/3 pound hand-patted creations, and a traditional smaller hamburger and cheeseburger. Add a patty, add chili, whatever combination you like.

The lead item on the menu is the Chuck Steak Sandwich. Chuck steak, in this case, is a country fried beef patty. Filling and hot.

The restaurant also features the Flavorburst machine with more than 30 different available flavors, plus shakes, floats, sundaes, freezes and a selection of Oreo ice cream creations.

372 Sebastian Street, Helena-West Helena * (870) 572-2271

127

THE HORNET DAIRY BAR

Place your order and wait for the cowbell! This longstanding town gathering place, named after the local high school mascot, does the traditional burgers-and-shakes routine while adding in plate lunches, catfish, sandwiches and big hunks of fresh-made pie. It's not uncommon to find homemade meatloaf, chicken spaghetti or even turkey and dressing on the specials menu. Desserts range from those thickly meringued pies to German chocolate cake, hot fudge cake and cobblers galore.

The restaurant's deli meat sandwiches are served hot or cold with your choice of cheese. Get a melt for extra special goodness. When your order's ready and you're waiting in your car, the cowbell will ring for your attention.

405 US Highway 70 West, Hazen * (870) 255-2235

HUGHES DRIVE-INN

The building has been a restaurant since the mid-1950s. The Hughes Drive-Inn has been family owned since 1972, with its large dining area, pull-under awning and classic signage.

Its big secret is one of the state's best dairy bar burgers, the Homestyle Burger, a hand-patted classic with onion and bell pepper notes, a juicy, perfectly griddle-cooked delight.

Being the only homegrown restaurant in town, it's no surprise that this eatery carries everything from pizza sticks and tuna sandwiches to "cheedar tots" (cheese-filled tater tots) and "beer rings" (beer battered onion rings), and Arkansas dairy bar staples like pizza burgers and a burrito deluxe. Add in a full breakfast menu and shakes, floats, sundaes and a dipped cone, and you can dine here all day, every day.

204 Fifth Street, Hughes * (870) 339-3200 * *cash only*

129

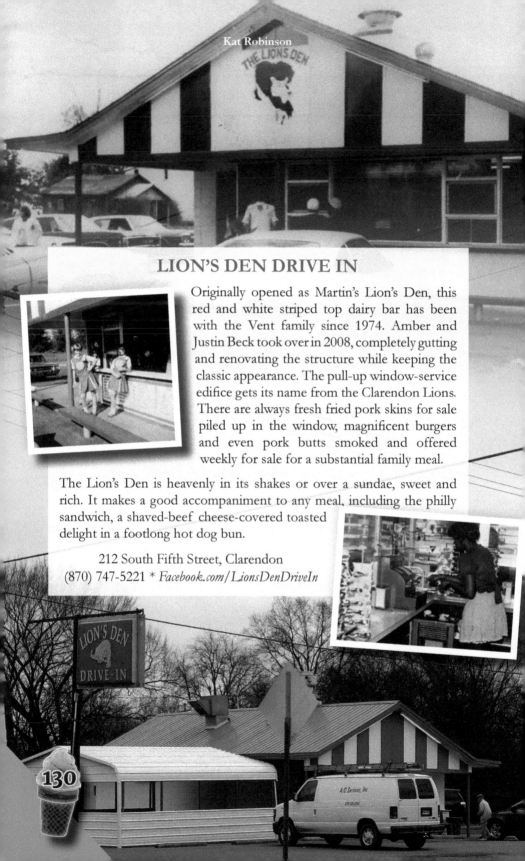

LION'S DEN DRIVE IN

Originally opened as Martin's Lion's Den, this red and white striped top dairy bar has been with the Vent family since 1974. Amber and Justin Beck took over in 2008, completely gutting and renovating the structure while keeping the classic appearance. The pull-up window-service edifice gets its name from the Clarendon Lions. There are always fresh fried pork skins for sale piled up in the window, magnificent burgers and even pork butts smoked and offered weekly for sale for a substantial family meal.

The Lion's Den is heavenly in its shakes or over a sundae, sweet and rich. It makes a good accompaniment to any meal, including the philly sandwich, a shaved-beef cheese-covered toasted delight in a footlong hot dog bun.

212 South Fifth Street, Clarendon
(870) 747-5221 * Facebook.com/LionsDenDriveIn

PIC-NIC-KER DRIVE IN

Mary Jenkins started the little brown dairy bar on the west side of Dumas back on July 4th, 1974. The stand is known for its griddle-smashed burgers, hot dogs and Polish - thick sausages served hot dog style - and for always having fruit punch and lemonade ready to consume from its constantly cascading machines.

646 West Waterman, Dumas * (870) 382-5091

132

RICH'S BURGERS

While other states have Krystal Burger and White Castle, there's just one place in Arkansas known for gutbomb-style griddle-smashed burgers you can purchase by the bag for less than a dollar each these days. That'd be here, at Richard Warriner Sr.'s original orange-trimmed stand just outside downtown Pine Bluff. Originally opened in 1961, Rich's menu has never been complicated - just burgers and fries, sandwiches and ice cream.

Warriner was an aviation mechanic who worked at the Aviation School at Grider Field south of the city during and after World War II. He was a pilot who owned several airplane of various vintage, and he'd sometimes give rides and sponsor air shows. That passion was also evident in the burger stand he opened and ran.

While a deluxe burger is available dressed how you like it, the original burger is just adorned with onion, pickle and mustard, savory rounds of beef between soft buns, quickly consumed, often in multiples. There's always a line when the shop is open, and during lunch both windows are hopping. Best to call in your order ahead.

Rich's also has one of the largest shakes available in the state - a half gallon of chocolate or vanilla, a ridiculous amount you'll want to share with a half-dozen friends.

102 North Walnut Street,
Pine Bluff
(870) 536-6950 * *cash only*

133

TROY'S DRIVE IN

In the heart of the Grand Prairie, in a town called DeWitt, one woman has taken on a family's established restaurant and made it all her own.

"When my business partner and I bought it, the people that had it before us had it for 37 years straight. They are the ones that named it Troy's. It comes from the husband, yes."

Stephanie Williams purchased the longstanding Troy's Drive-In in DeWitt in 2017. It had originally been built as the DeWitt Dairy Bar before being purchased in 1973 and renamed Troy's Drive-In.

"I was just a regular customer. It was always the favorite place to eat. You can look back in yearbooks in DeWitt High School and Troy's will always be the favorite place to eat in this town.

"Every fast food restaurant, which we only have two, I was there to open both of 'em, Sonic, and then Subway. The guy that was my business partner, he owned the Subway. He brought it to DeWitt. I managed it for him for eight years before we came over here. He owns a flying service - he's a pilot, crop-dusting pilot, and he just decided one day that he was done. So I was like, 'hey, I don't want to sell out. Let me buy you out.' And that's kinda how I got it."

"So why would you want to take on the operation of a dairy bar like this?" I ask.

"Because I love it. I love what I do. Food has always been my life, and then when I got here I could bring some of my own flavor to the menu, so hey, it was great, and I loved it. We just took off and it's been going ever since.

"We have almost everything that Na-dja and Troy had. We added the chicken wings, and we added barbecue nachos. We added stuff like that to bring just a little bit more of us into it. We just added the chicken wings about a year and a half. We fry 'em to order. Every time I go to a food show, if I see something I like, I'm bringing it back."

There's a singular dish that keeps people coming back to Stephanie's window.

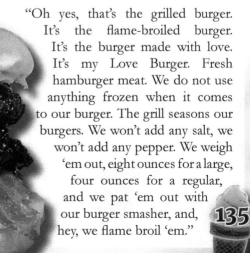

"Oh yes, that's the grilled burger. It's the flame-broiled burger. It's the burger made with love. It's my Love Burger. Fresh hamburger meat. We do not use anything frozen when it comes to our burger. The grill seasons our burgers. We won't add any salt, we won't add any pepper. We weigh 'em out, eight ounces for a large, four ounces for a regular, and we pat 'em out with our burger smasher, and, hey, we flame broil 'em."

135

"Sometimes those flames get pretty high!" I exclaim, catching the flourish of flame through the window, a full two, even three feet above the already elevated gas grill at the center of the cooking line.

"Oh, they get high, they get real high!" Stephanie answers. "It gets really hot in there. It's real hot, here come the flames! We have people that drive up just to see the flames."

My very first visit to Troy's in 2013, when I was working on *Classic Eateries of the Arkansas Delta*, I was sitting in my car with the air conditioning on, a hot July scorcher in full bloom, reading my messages on my phone when that burst of flame caught my eye. There were four people in the shop at the time, the temperature was nigh on 100 degrees outside and I could not imagine how anyone could manage to bear that sort of inferno. But when I got my burger at the window, and pulled it out sitting in my car, taking that photo, taking that first bite, I understood why it was so good, and why others chose to dine in their cars out front like I was. It was dinner and a show.

"What people like about it is the flame broil. It's the way we flip 'em on this grill, this gas grill," Stephanie shows me. "We got four burners that run down there, and it's gas, and we cook 'em just like if you were to have a charcoal grill outside."

The population of DeWitt, Arkansas is 3019 - which makes the amount of hamburger Stephanie uses each week truly extraordinary.

"Four or 500 pounds."

"Wait, what?"

"Yeah, so I get in 240 pounds every delivery, and I get two deliveries, sometimes more, so, you see that?" she says, showing me a patty on its wax paper, "that's what they like. Burgers are made every morning, 120 burgers every morning before we open up. Whatever we sell at lunch, we replace it, because we're probably gonna sell another 120 before 7:00. That's a lot of burgers for a little town, but they get double, triple meat, single meat, double burger with barbecue meat on it and an onion ring. They get a half a pound of barbecue meat put on top of a jumbo, double meat cheeseburger, and one big onion, 'cause, of course, our onion rings are so big. So you sit the onion ring on top of there, and don't forget the mayonnaise, pickle, lettuce, and tomato. But, yeah, we'll top a burger with pretty much anything. If you want fried mushrooms, fried pickles on your burger, jalapeño…"

I will note here, a Love Burger with battered and fried mushrooms is a sin I will confess to enjoying and will pay my penance for.

"We'll do same for a footlong," Stephanie continues. "We'll do the same for tater tots. We'll do same for French fries."

As we talk, cars continue to pull up, a steady stream that hasn't abated all afternoon. Most pull up to the window for call-ahead orders, but some pull in for window service. I guess our video rig has made people nervous, because there are four cars with folks in them, waiting patiently for us to clear out so they can walk up. I try to be helpful.

"Come on in here!" I holler, waving, while Stephanie grins, then notice the person who had been behind the car out on the road carried on. "Oh, they turned that way."

Stephanie just laughs.

Eventually, we're able to convince folks the walk-up window is open. Every person who walks up, Stephanie knows by name. She asks how they're doing, how their folks are.

"That's Steel, that's one of my favorites," she notes, pointing to a slender guy coming up to pick up his order. "He'll want to get out and get in front of the camera," she tells me. "Steel, he is definitely a regular."

"You come every day?" I ask.

"I try to, if I can afford it!" he responds, sending Stephanie into another gust of laughter.

"What do you like about this place?" Jeff Dailey, my cinematographer, asks.

"Everything! Best burger in southeast Arkansas!"

"I have people that come here that's moved away from here and been gone 30 or 40 years, and they come back and tell me they worked here for 25 cents an hour when they were teenagers," Stephanie relates. "And they cannot believe that it looks the same and that it's still here and it's still in operation. They can't, they just can't believe it.

"If somebody's from out of town and they get my number or look us up on Facebook and they want a burger, 'I'll be there in 10 minutes.' It's, 'No, this is a Love Burger. You've gotta be here in 15,' because we're not gonna run it through a conveyor belt. We're gonna cook your burger. It's gonna be hot, it's gonna be juicy, and it's gonna be fresh. It's gonna be good for you.

"Yeah, DeWitt loves Troy's. DeWitt means everything to Troy's. It means community. It means people coming together all the time, and not forgetting where you came from, and falling in love with something and being able to be in love with it for many years. I'm happy to be a part of that. I really am. I am."

1024 South Jefferson Street
(870) 946-1201

138

WHITE RIVER DAIRY BAR

Never advertised, just shared by word of mouth, this 50+ year old dairy bar on the old bridge road across the White River from downtown DeValls Bluff is still a destination of worth for duck hunters, fishing enthusiasts and locals in the area. Catfish is revered here, as are fried pies and the patty melt. The substantial yet humble burger is a solid go-to worthy of a detour.

The Brownie Surprise, a completely soft-serve covered fresh baked brownie topped with fudge, is an indulgent end to a filling meal.

7757 East Twin City Park Road, DeValls Bluff * (870) 998-7047

WILLY'S OLD FASHIONED HAMBURGERS

Housed in an '80's style sloped roof shack along Speedway Street in Dermott, Willy's has been a local favorite since its opening in 1986. Burgers here are salt-and-pepper spiced and generously applied with your condiments of choice. The marvelous ice cream shakes are made from hand-scooped and come in minimal flavors, but they're hearty. Vanilla is marvelous and my usual go-to.

Currently ran by Iqbal Singh, the eatery has become well known in the community not only for its burgers and shakes, but for the legendary "chicken box," which is a box packed to full with chicken strips, plus cheese sauce for dipping.

300 East Speedway Street, Dermott
(870) 538-5090

Lower Arkansas

South Central Arkansas

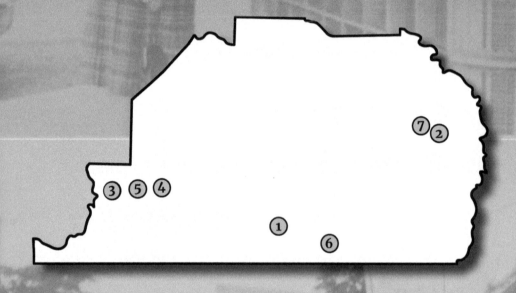

1. Betty's Old Fashion, El Dorado
2. Breaker Wheel Meals, Monticello
3. Burge's Smoked Turkeys and Hams, Lewisville
4. Jeff's Dairy Treet, Waldo
5. Jimmy's Drive In, Stamps
6. Ramona's City Grill, Strong
7. Ray's, Monticello

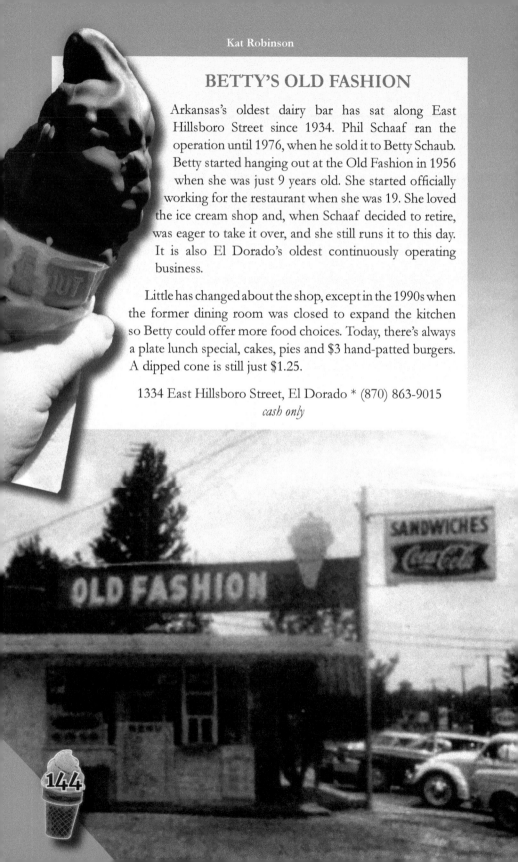

BETTY'S OLD FASHION

Arkansas's oldest dairy bar has sat along East Hillsboro Street since 1934. Phil Schaaf ran the operation until 1976, when he sold it to Betty Schaub. Betty started hanging out at the Old Fashion in 1956 when she was just 9 years old. She started officially working for the restaurant when she was 19. She loved the ice cream shop and, when Schaaf decided to retire, was eager to take it over, and she still runs it to this day. It is also El Dorado's oldest continuously operating business.

Little has changed about the shop, except in the 1990s when the former dining room was closed to expand the kitchen so Betty could offer more food choices. Today, there's always a plate lunch special, cakes, pies and $3 hand-patted burgers. A dipped cone is still just $1.25.

1334 East Hillsboro Street, El Dorado * (870) 863-9015
cash only

144

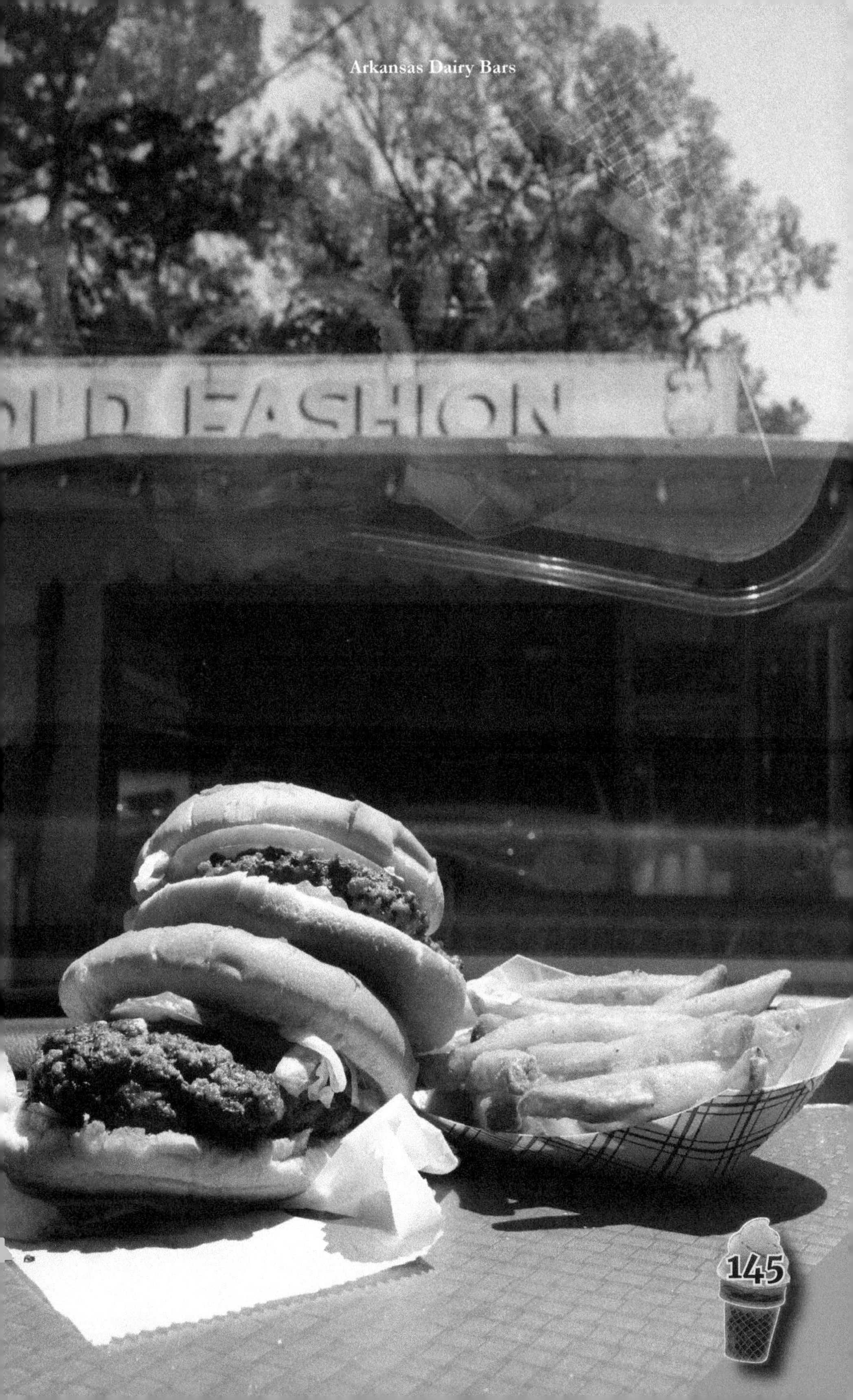
FASHION

BREAKER DRIVE IN

The last of a once 100 strong franchise out of Oklahoma, Monticello's location of the old Breaker Drive In is believed to be the last of its kind. Breaker Wheel Meals sprung up in the 1970s, including spots in Corning, Pocahontas, Little Rock, North Little Rock, and Monticello. Many were former Sonic locations; when Sonic struggled in the 1970s, it sold off property to the new fledgling chain, only to come back and open again in these cities, usually pretty near the Breakers Drive Ins in those previous spots.

The name came from popular 1970s slang and CB radio usage. The term "breaker" was used to cut in and begin a CB radio conversation. These drive ins had CB radios where drivers could place their orders on Channel 19 before they got to the restaurant - two decades before cell phones allowed drivers to do the same thing. The original logo had wheels at the front and back of the Breaker name to represent vehicles not, as some thought, roller skates, a Sonic Drive In hallmark.

Though the CB days are a memory, this location survives, offering excellent burgers and sundaes. Be sure to try the Polish, a common Lower Arkansas delicacy of a Polish sausage with the hot dog treatment.

523 West Gaines Street, Monticello * (870) 367-2942

147

BURGE'S SMOKED TURKEYS AND HAMS

Lewisville is home to one of the most iconic dairy bars in the state. It's been open since 1962, and it started with a guy smoking turkeys in his backyard.

"Alden Burge came to Lewisville in 1953 out of Shreveport," Deanna Porter tells me. "In 1962, he made a big decision and bought this place. The front half of it is the original half, and then as they grew, they had to keep adding on, so it kinda gives a little odd shape to it. But it's very unique and everybody recognizes it when they pass by."

Deanna manages the Lewisville location of Burge's Hickory Smoked Turkeys & Hams.

"It's not just turkeys and hams. We also have burgers, ice cream, barbecue, fish. Believe it or not, we have people drive from all over to eat our fish. Shreveport, Hope, from all over for our fish, which kinda surprises people.

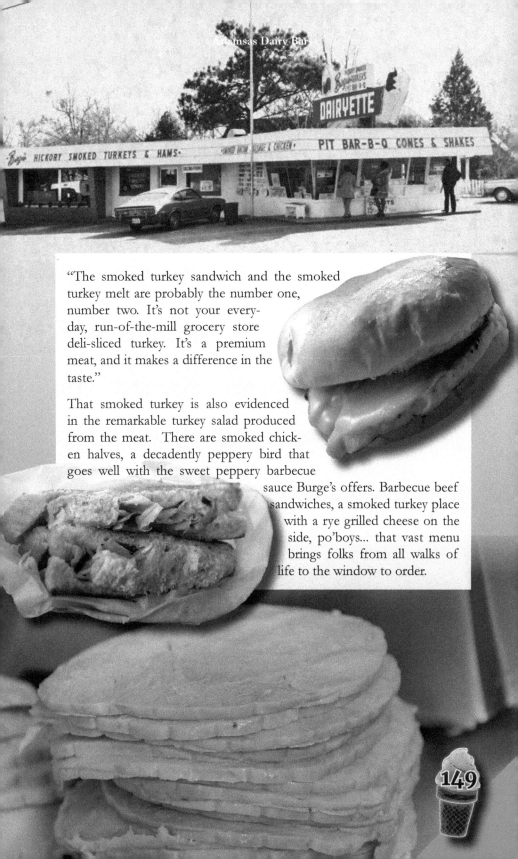

DAIRYETTE

Bozo's HICKORY SMOKED TURKEYS & HAMS· ·SMOKED BACON, SAUSAGE & CHICKEN· PIT BAR-B-Q CONES & SHAKES

"The smoked turkey sandwich and the smoked turkey melt are probably the number one, number two. It's not your every-day, run-of-the-mill grocery store deli-sliced turkey. It's a premium meat, and it makes a difference in the taste."

That smoked turkey is also evidenced in the remarkable turkey salad produced from the meat. There are smoked chicken halves, a decadently peppery bird that goes well with the sweet peppery barbecue sauce Burge's offers. Barbecue beef sandwiches, a smoked turkey place with a rye grilled cheese on the side, po'boys... that vast menu brings folks from all walks of life to the window to order.

149

There's a group of gentlemen dining in the back corner this afternoon, enjoying turkey melt sandwiches and peach pies. They're from Texarkana, thirty minutes away, but drop in every chance they get, which is often, since they fish nearby Lake Columbia and the Red River, and hunt on lands nearby in-season.

Out on the side of the building, a basketball team passing through the area is huddled around a metal picnic table, eating burgers and slurping shakes while huddling in matching gray uniforms. A couple and their daughter are at another table, digging into fries and sandwiches while the young one takes off her shoes and carefully arranges them on the table. Two men are walking up to the window after parking a truck and bass boat across the street. Log trucks hit their brakes and navigate the 90 degree turn at the stop sign out front.

And then there's Lesa Ray, who comes in to chat with me while waiting for her pickup order. I ask her how long she's been coming to Burge's.

"Fifty years!" she laughs. "I'm 56 years old, and we used to come up here every Sunday after church. There used to be a playground right over that

150

hill by the church, and we used to play at the playground and come to Burge's and get our lunch."

"Has it changed much?" I ask.

"It's still the same!"

"We'll see 'em, you know, four or five times a week," Deanna continues. "They'll come in and get their burgers, fries and shakes, and a day or so later, here, they come, 'It's Friday night, I gotta get my fish.' Or we'll see 'em getting their barbecue on the weekend, and we sell the stuff by the pound, as well. So they'll come and buy pounds of barbecue, beef, pork, whatever, you know, coleslaw, and they're going camping, they're going to the lake or fishing, and they gotta take their Burge's with 'em.

"The soft-serve ice cream has a lot to do with it. You know, a lot of places you go don't have that soft serve anymore. We have the vanilla, the chocolate, the twist. So we make the milkshakes, the banana splits, all the frosted drinks, that everybody remembers from years ago, we still do today."

"Ice cream, my sister, Bunny, loves it," Lesa laughs. 'I can't eat ice cream, but she always, as a kid, I would get a cone and she would get a cone. She would eat mine and then eat hers! Bunny loves ice cream from Burge's."

"We sell a lot of ice cream, a lot," Deanna shares. "Just about every order has a shake or an ice cream cone. Yeah, the summertime is very popular here."

The Burge's name is well known throughout the region as a powerhouse in holiday meats - in fact, Burge's website is literally SmokedTurkeys.com.

"November and December is, just for shipping alone, we'll ship around 10,000 or more packages in about six weeks," Deanna continues. "That doesn't count for what we sell in our restaurants.

"Everybody really appreciates the history and that it hasn't changed. So when they come here, they know what they're getting. We try to make sure everything tastes the same as it did 20 years ago if they stopped in here. And they'll tell you that. 'Nothing has changed,' 'it's exactly the way I remember when I come with my grandmother and my grandfather years ago,' and that's nice to hear. People go out of the way to come here from all over the United States."

Lesa sums up what Burge's really means to the community, before heading out the door with her order.

"If this place wants to leave, it'll be the last, in the whole town. It's really the last true business to stay. Yes, it is."

526 Spruce Street, Lewisville * (870) 921-4292 * *SmokedTurkeys.com*

152

153

JEFF'S DAIRY TREET

Elsie and Earl Rowe opened the tiny hamburger stand in Waldo back in the 1950s. The Rowes ran it for nearly 40 years before selling it to the Nowlins in the 1990s. Later, it became Buddy's Dairy Treet.

Jeff McClure, the son of Wade McClure who opened both of the Wade's Hamburger locations in Magnolia, bought the Dairy Treet in 2020 and only changed his name, keeping the tradition of the intentionally misspelled Treet on the sign. McClure's mom, aunts and cousins all worked at the restaurant growing up.

"The Cow," as it's called, gets its name from the large cow on the roof. That cow has been there for decades, except when it hasn't been. It's been the subject of pranks by high school students many, many times. Sometimes it appears in nearby pastures. Other times, it's shown up in backyards of surprised locals. When it's found, students take it right back to the Dairy Treet and put it back on top.

Jeff's one big change to the stand and to the cow itself has been to take it from its original paint job resembling a Jersey to a more Holstein appearance, recovering both stand and statue white with big black spots.

As far as the fare goes, it's classic dairy bar, with burgers and fried burritos, a bevy of potato options and loaded fries. The burgers - classic, hand-patted, nicely seasoned, griddle-smashed, juicy and fully dressed - are marvelous, a great homage to the burger stand's past. A note on the fried pickle chips - they're salty and portions are generous, so you'll want to share them quickly. Soft-serve ice cream, shakes and sundaes are always a nice touch.

216 West McKissick, Waldo * (870) 524-0040

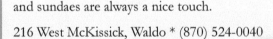

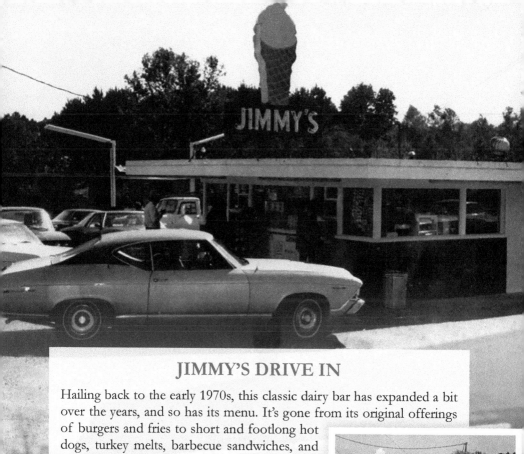

JIMMY'S DRIVE IN

Hailing back to the early 1970s, this classic dairy bar has expanded a bit over the years, and so has its menu. It's gone from its original offerings of burgers and fries to short and footlong hot dogs, turkey melts, barbecue sandwiches, and fried fish. The burgers are still a focus, as are frosteds, floats, shakes and Wizards (candy blended into soft-serve ice cream). Sandwiches come with chips unless you ask for something else. Generations of cruisers have pulled up, high schoolers from Waldo to Monticello, continuing an automotive tradition.

1207 East Antigo Street (US Highway 62), Stamps * (870) 533-2121

RAMONA'S CITY GRILL

A restaurant has to be willing to stand well behind their chili cheeseburgers when they offer an entire section's worth on their menu. While Ramona's offers four types each of its hamburgers and cheeseburgers, there are eight chili-related configurations of burgers, along with hot dogs, Frito pies and bowls served with crackers.

The chili, beanless and thick, swamps the ample burger here - you absolutely cannot pick this burger up without messing your shirt - but it's also hearty and warming..

95 East Second Avenue, Strong * (870) 797-7669

RAY'S

When you mention Monticello to someone from the town, chances are they're going to tell you come to this place to eat while you're here.

Ray's has a long legacy. C.L. Ray moved to Monticello in 1951 and got into the restaurant business with a place called The Anchor. Over the next few years he'd get another place that would take his name - and buy another joint that he named, hilariously, Andray's.

This iteration of his restaurant made its way to the corner of what's now Arkansas Highways 278 and 425, in 1964. Ray's son Mark took over in the mid 1970s. And then there's Chris Ray, Mark's son, who began managing the restaurant in 1997 and who owns the restaurant with his dad today.

"Our top sellers would be our barbecue, burgers, and catfish," Chris tells me, "those are our three main items, but we've got a very diverse menu. Salads, fried shrimp, chicken tenders, everything to tacos, with milkshakes, fried pies. We have a lot of different items, and everybody can find something to eat here.

"We still home-make a lot of items here. We smoke our barbecue. We make our own barbecue sauce, our baked beans, hand-bread onion rings every day, press out fresh hamburger meat every day, and make our coleslaw and tartar sauce, as well."

Indeed, Ray's has about anything you might want to eat. It's the people who make this restaurant go. The kitchen is large, and it's packed, with more than a dozen workers behind the counter to the back of the house, all hands on deck to serve the hundreds of people who pass through each day.

Chris takes me on a tour of the kitchen, from the front where all the orders come through to send out the windows and across the counter, to the cook lines where meat is sizzling on the griddle and catfish is being dropped into the fryer, and on back to the prep area, where Pearl Jones is preparing the day's onion rings.

"How long have you been working here at Ray's?" I ask Pearl.

"About, how many, Chris, about 40 years?"

"Off and on, probably 40 years, that's right," Chris answers.

159

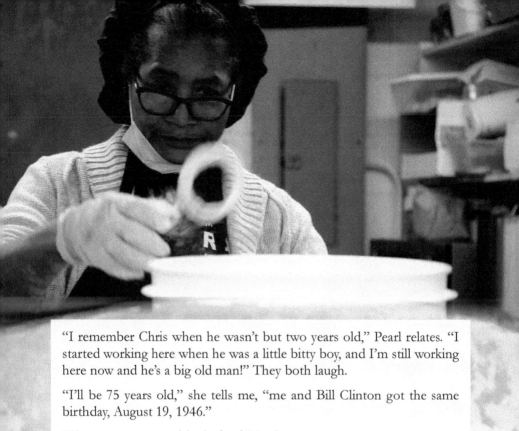

"I remember Chris when he wasn't but two years old," Pearl relates. "I started working here when he was a little bitty boy, and I'm still working here now and he's a big old man!" They both laugh.

"I'll be 75 years old," she tells me, "me and Bill Clinton got the same birthday, August 19, 1946."

"Have you ever seen him before?" I ask.

"Yeah, I've seen him. I'll tell you, he's been down here when he first got Governor. He's all right."

"Bill Clinton told my dad that those were the best baked beans that he's ever eaten," Chris speaks up.

"Bill Clinton said that? Wonder if it wasn't something I made!" Pearl chuckles. "My momma learned me how to cook. We had to do it."

Pearl keeps working… there's no stopping for a sit-down interview when onion rings need to be prepped for the day.

She walks me through the process.

"I'm making the stuff up to roll the onion rings," she starts. "You gotta make three buckets, and I put two eggs in the buckets, so I gotta beat them up. We put 'em in the flour, put 'em in the milk, the egg, back in the flour, just the cracker meal."

Curious, I ask, "why would you use cracker meal instead of something like cornmeal?"

"I don't know," she replies, "That's what Mark, his daddy, taught me. And his grandpa."

I let Pearl get on with the onion ring making, now happy to know the secret behind some of my favorite onion rings in the world.

Chris continues to show us around, chatting about other favorites from the restaurant.

"Yeah, we used farm-raised American catfish. It's a little more expensive to go that route, but we have a big following on fish. We used to have some fish buffets in town and they've fallen by the wayside, and so we kinda became the fish place here. We go through a lot of catfish. Approaching, like, 60 cases a week."

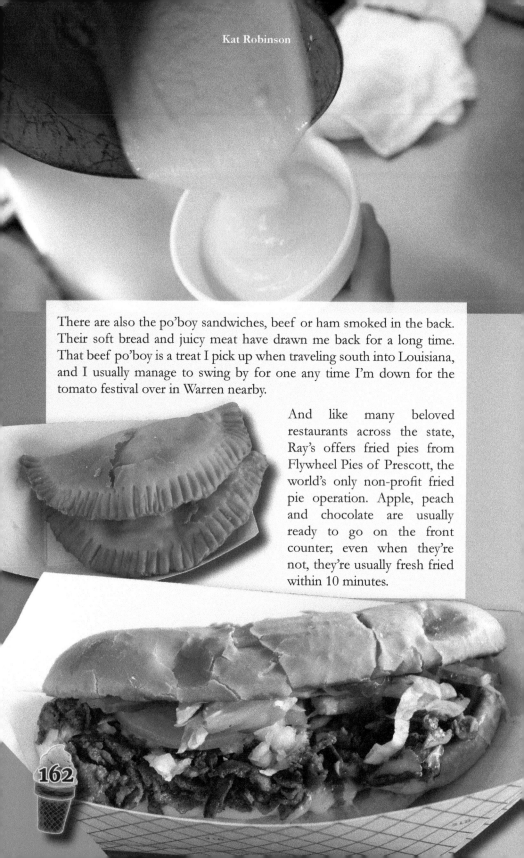

There are also the po'boy sandwiches, beef or ham smoked in the back. Their soft bread and juicy meat have drawn me back for a long time. That beef po'boy is a treat I pick up when traveling south into Louisiana, and I usually manage to swing by for one any time I'm down for the tomato festival over in Warren nearby.

And like many beloved restaurants across the state, Ray's offers fried pies from Flywheel Pies of Prescott, the world's only non-profit fried pie operation. Apple, peach and chocolate are usually ready to go on the front counter; even when they're not, they're usually fresh fried within 10 minutes.

"A lot of guys eat lunch in here every weekday, it seems like, and it's kind of a spot to come in and, you know, visit with other guys around town on the lunch break," Chris tells me.

"It's a popular hangout at lunch, I would say. It gets tough sometimes, but it's really been good to us and our family over the years, and I'm grateful I made the decision to get into the restaurant business."

207 US Highway 425, Monticello * (870) 367-3292
RaysHamburgers.com

163

Ouachitas

Southwest Arkansas

1. Bailey's Dairy Treat, Hot Springs
2. Dairyette, Mount Ida
3. The Dugout, Texarkana
4. Frosty Treat, Hot Springs
5. Herb's Creamland, Ashdown
6. Hope Dairy Freeze, Hope
7. Jerry's Drive In, Ashdown
8. King Kone, Hot Springs
9. Lighthouse Drive In, Wickes
10. Mel's Dairy Bar, Malvern
11. Myer's Cruizzers, Mena
12. Old Tyme Burger Shoppe, Texarkana
13. Pinky's Drive In, Delight
14. The Shack, Jessieville

BAILEY'S DAIRY TREAT

The history of this Art Deco dairy bar goes back to 1952, when it was originally opened as Butchie's. Within a few years, it gained a new name - the Polar B'ar - complete with a polar bear on top of the sign. Later on, it was the starting point of Rocky's Corner, an excellent pizza and Chicago foods restaurant now located across from Oaklawn Racing Park.

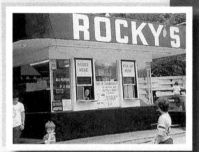

In the 1990s, the name was changed again, to Bailey's Dairy Treat. Lien Morphew purchased the business - which he had been working at for some time - in 1995. Today, he and his wife continue offering dairy bar delights along Park Avenue, six days a week.

"I came here from Vietnam in 1975," he tells me. "I'm adopted by an American family."

Lien was just 18 at the time. He graduated from Hot Springs High School in 1978. Since taking over Bailey's, he's grown a network of regulars who visit often, some weekly, some daily.

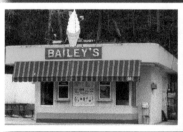

I ask him, what keeps people coming back?

"We are friendly. We treat anybody just like family. I make my own very fresh hamburger meat."

Bailey's goes through about 40 pounds of beef each day, all hand-patted and seasoned and cooked on the original grill in the back. While the burgers are good, they're not the only savory specialty offered.

"Real chicken fried rice and beef steak fried rice, and fried rice egg roll. I'm the only one to have it. My fried rice is just for anybody to have a chance to try something new."

It is absolutely splendid. I would never have thought to pair beef fried rice with ice cream, but the Morphews have perfected a recipe that perfectly combines the Asian rice and vegetables with a burger seasoned beef steak strip. It's delectable.

Of course, ice cream is the really big star here. It's common to see families with cones relaxing at the picnic tables on either side of the tiny hut.

"We have vanilla ice cream only, but we have banana splits, sundae, and shake," Lien tells me. He swiftly constructs one of the most popular delights, a banana split. "We make (ours) in a cup, not in a bowl. Chocolate, strawberry, and pineapple, with banana," he chuckles.

Though the Morphews' operation is just a few blocks from downtown and the famous Hot Springs Bathhouse Row, the majority of the clientele is locals returning often for their favorites.

"These burgers are great. Burgers are great, fries, good. It's always been good," says Justin Chambers, who says he comes by several times each week. "I've seen it go through several owners, but it's always been Bailey's, you know what I mean?"

"They say, 'Hey, Lien! I want two cheeseburgers! Good?' I say, 'Yes, we know what you want. Wait here.'" Lien giggles. His laughter is contagious.

"I've known some so long, they give me finger like that," he says, holding up his index finger, "I know what they want."

169

Another familiar face appears at the window next to the gigantic golden Buddha statue.

Lien lights up. "That's Larry! Larry Sanders!"

"Hey, Larry!" I call out.

"Hi, how are you!" he answers.

"I'm fine, just recording a TV show on dairy bars!"

Larry leans into the window, his eyes widening. "They have the best burger place in Hot Springs because it's homemade. Everything's, you know, the patties, everything's just perfect. Beautiful."

Thing is, Lien is probably his own best customer.

"I love my cook," he beams, talking about his wife, "so I eat everything. People say, 'Lien, why don't you go out to eat?' I say, 'Well, my food is good, too, so why go to somewhere and eat?' So I eat my own food here."

BAILEY'S DAIRY TREAT
"old fashion hamburgers"
— 624-4085 —

Bailey's most famous customer has been coming by for decades. As it turns out, Bill Clinton was friends with the folks that ran the Polar B'ar when he was in high school in the 1960s. He'd slide in the back door and sometimes help out making burgers and ice cream.

Lien says President Clinton has been by many times, and though the former president has recently gone vegan, he used to be a big fan of Bailey's chili cheeseburgers.

For Lien Morphew, there's just one secret to keeping Bailey's Dairy Treat going.

"We work hard, and then, when they come, we smile and treat them just like family."

510 Park Avenue, Hot Springs * (501) 624-4085

THE DAIRYETTE

Have you ever been crystal digging? Mount Ida, Arkansas, is the world's quartz crystal capital. It's also home to Camp Ozark, which draws hundreds of youngsters each summer. It also sits on the southwest corner of Lake Ouachita - Arkansas's largest lake, so clean and pristine that you can see your feet when you're neck deep. Good fishing, great vacationing, and prime eating if you love a good dairy bar.

"George McClerkin and his wife built it in 1953, and they started selling food out of it in 1958. It was passed down to Harley Ferguson. He bought it in the '70s, and he ran it all the way into 1986. They sold it to Abernathys, and Joyce had the opportunity to buy this, and this was her, I mean, this was her goal, was to own her own business and to own the Dairyette."

Adam O'Neal started at the Dairyette in 2012. He became general manager in 2020. His mom, Joyce, bought the restaurant in 2000.

"She's pretty much made the tradition stronger than it ever has been," Adam tells me. "My mom remembers when she was seven years old, coming up here and getting a banana split. It's amazing to come as a child at that age and to think that, one day, you might be the owner of that."

The restaurant retains much of its original charm. There are still hand-written signs for the flavors of shakes and sundaes that hail from the early days of the restaurant.

"We don't want to lose that. It's nice to roll through those doors and to kinda step back in time, a little bit. It is still nice that there's places out there, even being in the little town of Mount Ida."

Whichever way you approach on US Highway 270, the iconic neon-lit ice cream cone on a pole at the corner of the building is one of the first things you see.

"In 1976, Harley Ferguson, the ice cream outside, he had sold it," Adam relates. "His niece worked here. She begged him and begged him, so Harley ended up having to go and pay more for the ice cream cone than actually sold it, just to get it back in the same day."

The Dairyette is open year round. During the colder months, it's mostly locals making up the clientele, but on any summer day you can meet someone from just about anywhere.

Kat Robinson

"It's a lot of people that come in from different parts of the world with camp, but also just people just traveling, you know, kinda living that American dream, and this is kinda part of it, all the way from Germany, England, Czech Republic. A lot of it is families coming through, you know, enjoying life, because this is a very outdoors community."

The menu is vast.

"We sell a lot of chicken - it's probably with chicken strips, our tenders, popcorn chicken. We have chicken-fried steak. We have chicken-fried chicken. We sell a lot of wraps with our chicken. We sell a lot of salad with our grilled chicken."

"And lots of dogs?" I confirm.

"Oh, like, yes. Lots of dogs. We do shakes, that's what we're known for, and we can make just about any shake, any topping we have. We do sundaes, we do floats, we do blenders. Just about any mixers. One of the signatures is the regular, just old-school ice cream cone. Man, it don't get no better than that."

174

Dairyette employees are taught how to roll the cone under the ice cream just right to be able to stack cones tall and beautifully.

When it comes to the classics, though, you can't beat a burger.

"The cheeseburger and probably shoestring fry. That's been on the menu since this place has been here," Adam tells me.

And he's not wrong. Burgers fry on the griddle under a watchful eye so as to never char black. Cheese is heated on the griddle and then spread across the patty, which ensures that it's fully melted by the time it's wrapped. Care is taken throughout the dressing of each burger, with condiments being spread fully across the bun in a thin layer. Every addition, from lettuce and tomato to add-ons like bacon, is done deliberately. Most of all, care is taken to ensure the burger isn't crushed when it's wrapped, so you get the sandwich's full thickness.

SHAKES

VANILLA
STRAWBERRY
CHOCOLATE
CHERRY
ORANGE
BANANA
PINEAPPLE
BUTTER SCOTCH
PEANUT BUTTER
COKE
DR PEPPER

SUNDAES

CHOCOLATE
CHERRY
STRAWBERRY
BUTTER SCOTCH
PINEAPPLE
HOT FUDGE

The Dairyette manages to thrive because of a commitment to quality, consistent preparation, and excellent ingredients, whether that's in the perfect lettuce leaf, the crispiest fries, or the marvelously presented banana split that's earned a reputation as the best in the state.

Adam says The Dairyette isn;t just a place you expect to get an instant meal. It takes time.

"This isn't fast food, this is real food, and everything's hand-cut. We cut this just for you. It's real beef. It's real onions. It's butter leaf lettuce. We pride ourselves off of it. There's no shortcuts here, just hard work and dedication.

"We don't have a Dairyette in every town or every state, but if we did, then it wouldn't be what it is today. It wouldn't be special, and you gotta come to Mount Ida to get it."

717 Highway 270 East, Mount Ida
(870) 867-2312 * *Facebook.com/MyDairyette*

THE DUGOUT

David Oliver's crazy idea for a sports-themed restaurant came to fruition as his family's own business back in 2015. Now, recently moved into the former Tamolly's space in the same shopping center, there's twice as much dining space to enjoy the span of burgers, hot dogs and shakes. The star of the show is the selection of 13" all-beef hot dogs in so many variations, like The Change Up, a 13 inch all beef wiener topped with tator tots, chili, cheese, cheese dip, jalapeños, onions, and mustard. If Frito pies are also a love, go for the Dodger Dog which is all that plus Fritos. Each dog is big enough for two.

3809 East 9th Street, Suite 5, Texarkana * (870) 330-4109
TheDugout15.com

FROSTY TREAT

Originally opened in 1951 and named the Fros-T-Treat, this slant-windowed shack along East Grand Avenue was relaunched in 2014 as the Frosty Treat under the eye of Lain Rodgers. Today, the proceeds from sales at the shop go to fund Shalom Women's Center, a faith-based non-profit for at-risk women. The restaurant has long served a fantastic housemade veggie burger, but in the past decade has also added vegetarian hot dogs, corn dogs, and even chili. Of course, the Frosty Treat has ice cream, too, and does a mean chocolate vanilla twist cone.

1020 East Grand Avenue, Hot Springs * (501) 609-0130
Facebook.com/FrostyTreatHotSprings

179

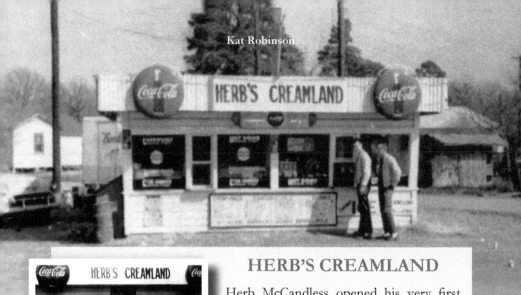

HERB'S CREAMLAND

Herb McCandless opened his very first restaurant on May 1, 1954 at the corner of Dupree and Highway 71 and Ashdown. It was a drive-up with a couple of windows where folks could come up and order a Herb Burger, root beer or an ice cream cone. Herb's original restaurant was one of a nationwide chain of ice cream stands known as Zesto, an ice cream and custard concept created by L.A.M. Phelan with Taylor Freezer Corporation in 1945; by 1955, Taylor Corp. had abandoned the idea, leaving a string of independent operators across the United States.

Herb ran that two-window walk-up along with a Gulf station in the 1950s. In 1965 he moved to a larger dairy bar with a big awning, where you could pull your car in under for some shade. He also had a car wash, taking advantage of having young driver clientele who would spend hours on his property enjoying burgers, milkshakes and fellow young folks. Yearbook ads for the restaurant featured the tagline "We cater to students," and it showed.

In the 1980s, Herb added pizza and moved into a larger building with a dining area on Dutch Webster Road, where the restaurant is located today. There are plate lunches and Herb burgers, fried okra and squash and onion rings and such, and deli sandwiches. After Herb's passing in 2014, the Randy Dandy - a dressed and stacked ham, turkey and cheese sandwich - was renamed the Herby Dandy. Shakes, floats, cups and cones are still sweet and delicious.

116 Dutch Webster Drive, Ashdown * (870) 898-2200

181

HOPE DAIRY FREEZE

Originally opened as a Dairy Queen in the 1950s, this location has seen generations of Hope students pulling ice cream cones and working Char-Burgers on the grill. In 2010, the independent shop switched names to become the Dairy Freeze, with the same but growing menu. Stop in for a Thousand Island Burger, or a turkey melt. The eatery has become well known for having some of the city's best fried catfish. Desserts are all ice-cream based, from freeze milkshakes to the Caramel Pecan Fudge Supreme; frozen coffee and slushes are a nice, refreshing choice for hot days.

917 East Third Street, Hope * (870) 777-4201
Facebook.com/HopeDairyFreeze

JERRY'S DRIVE IN

Originally opened by Jerry Haskins in a former Sonic Drive-In in 1977, Jerry's has served Ashdown for decades with righteous hot dogs, good burgers, Cajun fare, and all manners of tasty fare. The bright neon along Constitution Avenue leads diners to curbside intercom service under outstretched awnings and what might be southeast Arkansas's most densely packed menu board.

In addition to a delightfully thick set of selections of ice cream and burgers, there's a whole column dedicated to "fun foods" such as Natchitoches meat pies, fried green beans, fried ravioli, chicken crispitoes and pork eggrolls. There are also some of the most massive footlong hot dogs I've discovered anywhere, based on a 1/3 pound Nathan's all-beef wiener, that's tasty and remarkably filling.

Sundaes and ice cream delights like the Chocolate Sin-Sation are smoothly marvelous.

Jerry's also happens to be Arkansas's only combination liquor store and dairy bar, and while the two for the most part don't mix, you can order non-alcoholic frozen beverages that also work well as mixers.

1210 South Constitution Avenue, Ashdown
(870) 898-2244 * *Facebook.com/JerrysDriveIn8982244*

183

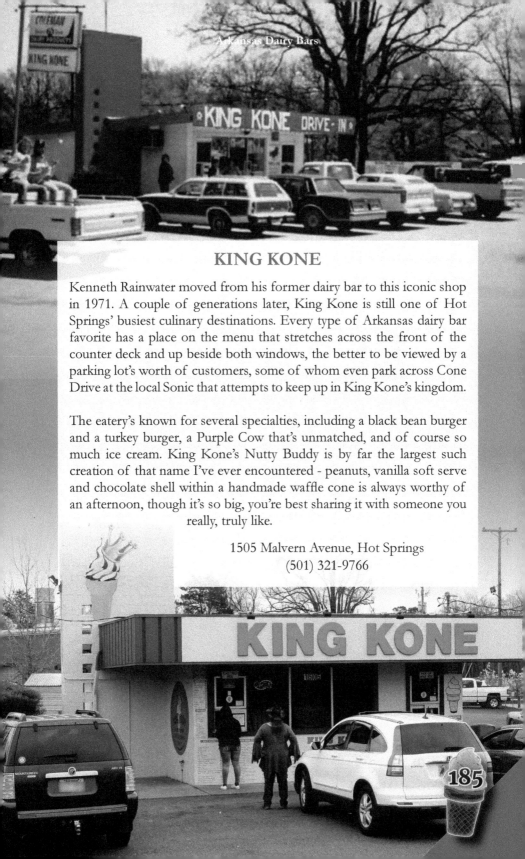

KING KONE

Kenneth Rainwater moved from his former dairy bar to this iconic shop in 1971. A couple of generations later, King Kone is still one of Hot Springs' busiest culinary destinations. Every type of Arkansas dairy bar favorite has a place on the menu that stretches across the front of the counter deck and up beside both windows, the better to be viewed by a parking lot's worth of customers, some of whom even park across Cone Drive at the local Sonic that attempts to keep up in King Kone's kingdom.

The eatery's known for several specialties, including a black bean burger and a turkey burger, a Purple Cow that's unmatched, and of course so much ice cream. King Kone's Nutty Buddy is by far the largest such creation of that name I've ever encountered - peanuts, vanilla soft serve and chocolate shell within a handmade waffle cone is always worthy of an afternoon, though it's so big, you're best sharing it with someone you really, truly like.

1505 Malvern Avenue, Hot Springs
(501) 321-9766

THE LIGHTHOUSE DRIVE IN

I believe this longstanding spot along US Highway 71 between De Queen and Mena may be the only such dairy bar in Arkansas that started as a motor court. First opened in 1952 as Sybil Bishop's Lighthouse Cafe, a 24-hour a day operation for the Lighthouse Courts Motel, the business became a drive inn when purchased by A.J. and L.A. Robinson in the 1960s. The business passed to their nephew and his wife, Bob and Linn Robinson, in 1999. The Penningtons took over in 2010.

The Lighthouse property has also been home to a gas station and car wash. Most of the structures are long gone, but the lighthouse still stands, quite some distance from the dairy bar itself. I've noted many times watching people pull in just to get their photo with the creation.

Lighthouse Cafe and Courts

MIDWAY BETWEEN DeQUEEN AND MENA

CLEAN • MODERN

Old ads note the eatery's burgers, shakes, "seafood and delights," and today, many of those items remain, including what's called a Hog Head burger, and the Hippo Burger - the latter of which being a gigantic feast of a burger meant for sharing. A fish plate and shrimp plate represent the seafood from that time. There's a statement on the menu by the Mexican fare - "We put jalapeño juice in our cheese," diners are warned, with selections including pork street tacos and Ugly Nachos.

The Lighthouse offers smoked pork butt barbecue, too, straight from its big canister smoker overlooked by a metal Roadrunner statuette out front. Sometimes chicken is also smoked. As far as the plate lunches, they include chicken strips and steak fingers - both of which are served with gravy, toast and French fries.

More than 20 different shake flavors are offered, thanks to the Flavorburst system. You can also enjoy sundaes, floats, malts, and limeades here.

7176 US Highway 71, Wickes * (870) 385-2313

MEL'S DAIRY BAR

Melvin Hallie Efird started the humble dairy bar beloved to generations of Malvern High students back in 1969 and ran it for more than 34 years. The business he began still runs strong just southwest of downtown. Though there's no sign by the road, you can find the yellow three-window edifice always with several cars under the awning.

Little has changed in the more than 50 years since Mel's first opened. You can still get a shake or malt to go with your meal, whether it's a barbecue sandwich, ham sandwich, chicken sandwich or hot dog. If you're looking for an epic choice to share with your date, go for the Triple Jumbo Cheeseburger - it's about a pound and a half, enough for two, thick hand-patted patties with cheese in-between on a bun just sturdy enough to contain the savory. Just be sure to ask for napkins, because Mel's burgers are so very juicy.

1228 Stanley Street, Malvern * (501) 337-0696

189

MYER'S CRUIZZERS

Don and Judye Myer's moved from Fort Smith to Mena in 1975 and took over running a Sonic Drive-In. Wanting to offer their own food items, the Myer's broke away from the chain, starting Myer's Cruizzers and solidifying their intercom-order business into a community favorite.

The Myer's three children, Cotye, Brandi and Justin, all grew up in the operation and eventually stepped in to manage and run the business. It still retains gorgeous purple and green neon and a yard of bright tables and cans on the property.

Myer's offers a stupendous selection of dairy bar foods. Its burgers are griddle-smashed, hot dogs are seared, cones are dipped thickly, shakes are...

Well, let's talk about those shakes, shall we? Because shakes are what got me into Myer's the first time about a dozen years back. Grav and I were out and about, seeking good food finds in the proximity of Queen Wilhelmina State Park. It was August, it was near 100 degrees, and we needed something cool and refreshing.

What we got was an overwhelming menu board of ice cream delights, including, I kid you not, all these shake flavors: strawberry, strawberry cheesecake, mocha, chocolate, vanilla, turtle, butterscotch, banana, peanut butter, pineapple, blueberry pie, and hot fudge - all of which are also offered malted. Throw in the slush flavors - grape, orange, tutti frutti, lime, coconut, margarita, cherry, banana, cotton candy, pina colada, lemon, peach, blue raspberry, watermelon, candy apple, limeade and anything combination therein for floats and frosted drinks, too, plus root beer, cherry phosphates and fresh squeezed lemonade. You will be cool after dining here.

Myer's also does an excellent take on the Polish that's common in Lower Arkansas - with its Cruizzer's Sandwich, a split hot Polish sausage with Ranch dressing and Swiss cheese on a dressed and toasted Hoagie bun.

409 Highway 71 North, Mena * (479) 394-5550.

OLD TYME BURGER SHOPPE

The original restaurant, opened by Bobbie and Debbie Grammer in 1988, was bought by Tom Collins and Randy Thomas in 1991. Collins - who also at one time or another ran Tombo's BBQ, Texas Burger, and The Hushpuppy - convinced Thomas to buy in with him, beginning a 30 year partnership that would continue on with their sons, Thomas Collins and Justin Thomas. Over the years, the owners' parents made pies, and the younger men and subsequent generations grew up in the store. Today, it's owned by Kenneth and Jarra Parris, who purchased the restaurant in 2021.

The burgers on the marquee always come with a perfectly toasted bun, hand-patted patties and choice of condiments. Regulars come in for a good old-fashioned country breakfast, and there's a daily meat-and-two lunch special. The veggie plate is a common order, as is the legendary chicken fried steak. Beans, stew, and chili are all offered with cornbread. There are also a lot of pies - cream pies, fried pies, meringue pies and whatever comes to mind on a particular day.

When it comes to ice cream, you can have your ice cream by itself, in a float or in a shake - particularly a magnificent peanut butter shake.

1205 Arkansas Boulevard, Texarkana * (870) 772-5775 * *oldtymeburger.com*

192

PINKY'S DRIVE IN

For more than 50 years, this double window dairy bar (formerly Pinkey's Drive Inn) has served the tiny community known as the birthplace of famed musician Glen Campbell. While the burgers and cones are well known, it's a fantastic cooked-to-order from scratch country fried steak that should be on your ticket - served with mashed potatoes, choice of gravy, salad, and hot dog bun garlic bread - is absolutely worth the 20 minute wait. All food made when you order, like good country food should be.

404 Antioch Road, Delight
(870) 379-2611

193

THE SHACK

In my opinion, one of the very best plates of catfish you can find in the entire state of Arkansas. The crew at this Jessieville mainstay expertly handle their fish, so lightly breaded. Two piece with salad. Fried pies on the counter soft serve machines brick and glass enclosure.

But there's so much more at The Shack. For instance, the Larry Special, two hamburger patties with grilled onions, French fries, slaw and a roll is a popular and substantial lunch. Or any number of burgers, chicken strips, fried burritos, fried mushrooms, fries and the like - the menu is thick. And for dessert, there are fried pies, banana splits, brownie hot fudge sundaes, and ICBs (which I believe stand for Ice Cream Blends).

It's the catfish, though, that's kept this beautifully designed restaurant going since 1972.

The Shack is good any time, but I'd suggest timing so you don't arrive or depart when school is letting out - the high school is right across the street.

7901 North Highway 7, Jessieville * (501) 984-5619

194

Central

Central Arkansas

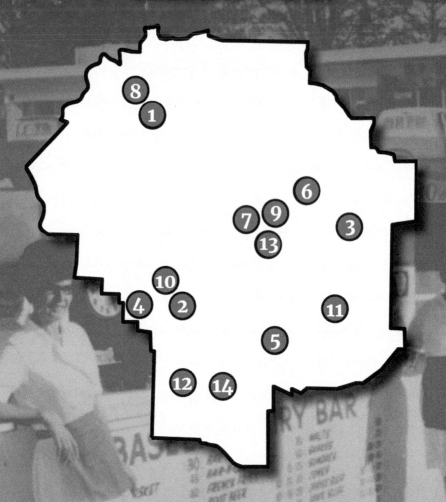

1. Atkinson's Blue Diamond Cafe, Morrilton
2. Garry's Sling Blade, Benton
3. Jackrabbit Dairy Bar, Lonoke
4. Kream Kastle, Benton
5. Mammoth Orange Cafe, Redfield
6. Minute Man, Jacksonville
7. Mojo's Dairy Bar, North Little Rock
8. Morrilton Drive In Restaurant, Morrilton
9. The Original Scoop Dog, North Little Rock
10. Salem Dairy Bar, Benton
11. Spradlin's Dairy Delight, England
12. The Whippet Family Restaurant and Drive In, Prattsville
13. Wink's Dairy Bar, North Little Rock
14. Yellow Jacket Drive In, Sheridan

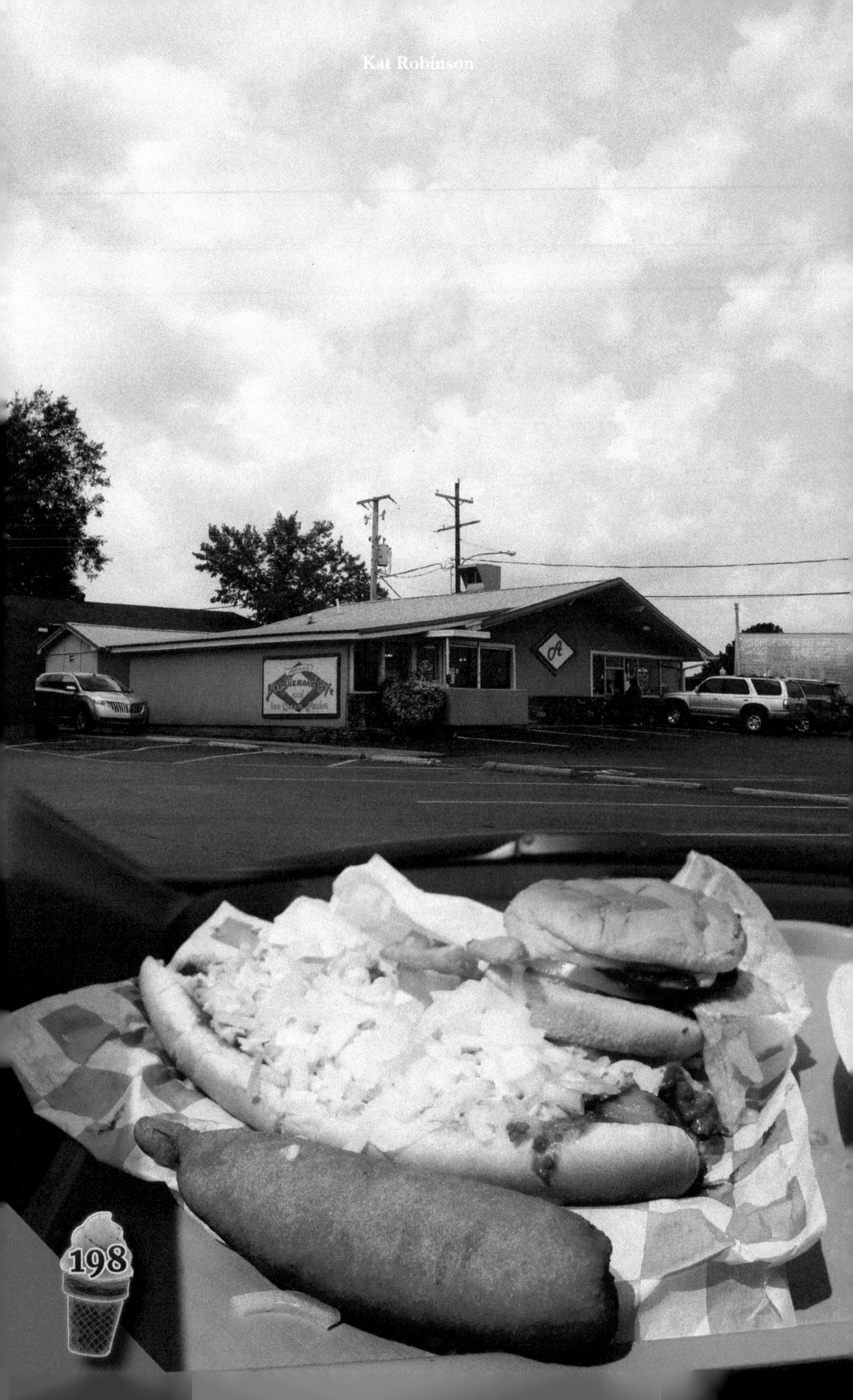

ATKINSON'S BLUE DIAMOND CAFE

A popular dairy bar all the way back to the 1970s, this orange building on the east side of town near Interstate 40 still draws the locals. It was purchased in 2004 by two couples, Gary and Karen Atkinson, and Earl and Pat Eichenberger. It's part family restaurant, part old fashioned ice cream parlor, and all good eats.

There are a whole lot of dishes I could suggest, from the really good cheese dip to the textbook example of a fried pickle chip.. The sandwiches and burgers are all worthy of note.

However, there's one dish that's truly signature here, and perfect for the place where it's offered. That'd be the Dandy Dog, a corn dog made to order with fresh batter. At its center, a Petit Jean hot dog - not just any variety, but the classic red skinned dog beloved by so many. Petit Jean Meats is located about a quarter mile away from Atkinson's Blue Diamond Cafe, and its influence is felt throughout the menu and even in the name and logo for the restaurant itself.

Not to be missed - ice cream delights, such as an honest to goodness ice cream sandwich made with soft-serve and fresh baked chocolate chip cookies - a real winner.

1600 East Harding Street, Morrilton
(501) 354-4253 * *TheBlueDiamondCafe.com*

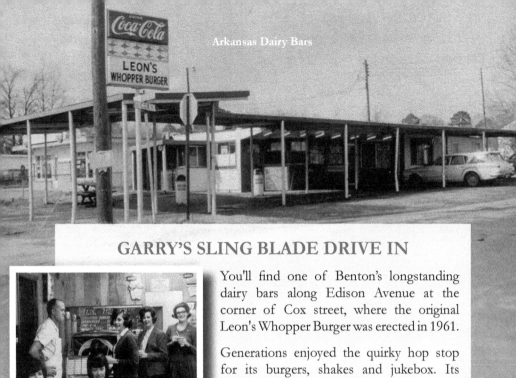

GARRY'S SLING BLADE DRIVE IN

You'll find one of Benton's longstanding dairy bars along Edison Avenue at the corner of Cox street, where the original Leon's Whopper Burger was erected in 1961.

Generations enjoyed the quirky hop stop for its burgers, shakes and jukebox. Its combination of walk-up service, soda counter and intimate booths made it a spectacular teenage hangout.

Leon's Whopper Burger was owned and operated by Leon and Louise Patterson. It was one of two Whopper Burger locations in Benton - the other being on old Military Road. Benton had an affinity for dairy bars through the 60s into the 90s, with Ruff's Tastee Freeze, a Dairy Queen, the Congo Road station that became the Salem Dairy Bar, Hickey's Dairy Cone on the Little Rock Highway and the Kream Kastle on the way out towards Hot Springs. The town's population seemed particularly adoring of these establishments.

LONG HOT DOG   85   PIZZA BURGER   60   ONION RINGS   45   FLOATS
AMBURGER REG.   40   HOT DOG   40   HOT TURNOVERS   25   MILK
AMBURGER DELUXE   50   STEAK REG   with ICE CREAM   30
EESEBURGER   ICE CR

In the 1980s, the Pattersons's daughter Peggy Wilson and her husband Garry, took on the restaurant, and ran it for a couple of decades. The restaurant dropped the Whopper Burger name after Burger King contacted Garry and his kin and pointed out that the name "Whopper" was now a trademarked item. At that point, the name was simplified to Garry's Drive In.

From around 2009 to 2014, Bob and Scottie Viall operated the restaurant, renaming it The Dairy Barn. Don and Cathy Huckaby purchased it in 2015 The Huckaby's had previously been in the grocery business in Malvern (Huckaby is a common name in this area of the state). Though Don passed away in 2019, the family still owns and runs the operation.

The name of the restaurant comes from the 1996 film *Sling Blade*, written and directed by Benton native Billy Bob Thornton, who won an Academy Award for best actor for his portrayal of Karl Childers. Thornton has no involvement in the operation. From what I've been told, the Huckabys decided to both invoke the recognizable Garry's name and that of the popular movie. The combination has been a hit, particularly with traveling film-goers who seek out movie locations.

Even now, though, folks refer to the place as the Whopper Burger, Garry's, or The Dairy Barn - depending on when they became associated with the restaurant. I just remember it as the red dairy bar at the end of Cox Street.

Whatever the name, the location draws lots of folks, not just from around the region but around the neighborhood, and for good reason. The eatery reeks of nostalgia, from its small number of bar stools to its three booths, the walls bedecked with every bit of dairy bar culture, Sling Blade stills and signage it can possibly muster. The south end of the restaurant is a packed kitchen with a classic dairy bar walk up window on the end; an addition from the 1980s offers a very busy drive-up window for call-in orders.

The Huckabys' biggest contribution to the legacy, outside of the new name, is probably the dedication the family to have local products available. When tomatoes are in season, they're absolutely fresh, as is other produce. Behind the counter, there are oodles of jars of jellies and the like, along with Juanita's brittles from Arkadelphia. Coolers offer a variety of bottled beverages, in case you'd rather get the true old-style counter-service feel of cold glass over what's pulled from the fountain.

The menu, like so many of our dairy bars across Arkansas, has grown with the time. While early iterations include cheeseburgers, footlong hot dogs, pork tenderloin sandwiches and the ubiquitous pizza burger, more recent additions are available, such as catfish and shrimp po'boys, Philly cheesesteaks, and even pizza.

The gold standard is a dressed cheeseburger seasoned lightly, griddle fried, American cheese melted on before being transferred to a light-ly toasted bun. Fries are crispy crinkle-cut, an Americana style pairing that's been steady to the\ location since at least the 1970s. It's pretty much the exact same burger you would have received if you'd ordered it two generations earlier.

But I have to brag outright on the strawberry shake. Instead of today's norm of a flavored syrup blended into soft serve, Garry's uses actual sliced and sugared strawberries with its milk and ice cream, creating a throwback confection full of delightful nostalgia.

619 Cox Street, Benton * (501) 776-8484

THE JACKRABBIT DAIRY BAR

This local hangout has gone through quite a few iterations over the decades since it opened in the 1960s. It was Bowden's Dairy Bar up through the second half of the 20th century, and Tidwell's Dairy Bar for most of the early 21st. And these days, it's the Jackrabbit Dairy Bar.

It's great to enjoy a good burger or ice cream, particularly dipped ice cream cones at this two-window walk-up. What's particularly awesome here is the cheese dip, a feature for decades. Want to guild that lily? Go for a fully dressed hot dog, where that all-beef wiener is covered in chili, onions, slaw, peppers, and cheese dip. You can't really pick it up with your fingers but hey, that's what a fork is for!

Recently, when footlong paper containers became scarce, that menu was altered. Now you can get a single, double or triple dog dressed out the same way.

Of course, when you have good cheese dip, you should have more things to put that cheese dip on. The Jackrabbit doesn't disappoint, with nachos, burritos, tacos, and chili cheese fries all with cheese dip on top or on the side.

511 West Front Street, Lonoke * (501) 676-2812

205

KREAM KASTLE DRIVE-IN

For years, I didn't know the name of this place on the way to Hot Springs. It was just the dairy bar on the side of the road where people ate. There were always cars parked around the building when it was open, and on the rare times I dropped in, I could count on a good burger and fries.

Turns out, Kream Kastle (or Kream Castle, as I have found it to be listed in old phone books half the time) opened in 1966 and has kept up a solid clientele to this day

A fine and regular selection of burgers, sandwiches, catfish dinners, smoked ribs and pork barbecue are standards at this roadside stand. The restaurant's potato salad also contains some of that finely shredded pork butt.

A standout is the patty melt sandwich - beautifully buttered and caramelized on the grill, almost translucent and redolent, unlike many patty melts, of cheese on both side of the meat.

Shakes are thick, sundaes are generous, and just about everyone in your family will find something good to eat here.

15922 US Highway 70, Benton * (501) 939-2350

MAMMOTH ORANGE CAFE

Inspired by the Frank E. Pohl Giant Orange Cafes in California, Ernestine Bradshaw opened the Mammoth Orange Cafe in 1960 along the Dollarway in Redfield. Three generations later, her grandson Jock Carter has assembled a crew to carry on the tradition of burgers and sundaes, along with daily lunch specials, served both inside and outside the definitive edifice.

Burgers are spot-on affairs, and ice cream a certain delight, but you'll want to make sure to save room for some of Jock's marvelously rendered barbecue if it's on the day's menu.

103 Arkansas Highway 365 North, Redfield
(870) 397-2347

MAMMOTH ORANGE

EX 7-2941

Variety of Sandwiches

Shakes-Sundaes
Alaska Size Hamburgers
Fountain Service

Redfield

MINUTE MAN RESTAURANTS

One of Arkansas's newest dairy bars is actually one of Arkansas's most beloved, nearly lost restaurant chains.

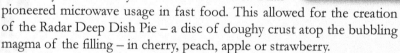

Wesley T. Hall's original Minute Man restaurant came out of a 24 hour coffee shop he owned with two other partners at 407 Broadway in Little Rock, way back in 1948. Eight years into the operation, he bought out his partners and converted the place into a hamburger joint. Soon, he had franchised out the Minute Man name and product across the state and even further – to seven states and 57 locations.

Hall's first restaurant was one of three in the nation to receive brand new microwave "Radar Ranges" from Raytheon to try out – and Minute Man pioneered microwave usage in fast food. This allowed for the creation of the Radar Deep Dish Pie – a disc of doughy crust atop the bubbling magma of the filling – in cherry, peach, apple or strawberry.

He was good at figuring out what people wanted and got them to buy those things from his store - not just with good food, but with good marketing. Back in 1975, he teamed up with the Coca-Cola company to do something revolutionary – offer a real glass with the Minute Man logo with a drink purchase.

1975 was also the year the Magic Meal was patented. It may be hard for some of you younger folks to believe, but used to be if you wanted to order something for your kid, it came off the same menu as the adults used. Minute Man sold Magic Meals two years before McDonald's began selling and promoting the Happy Meal (Minute Man would eventually sell the rights to sell Magic Meals to Burger King in the 1980s).

Minute Man also beat McDonald's to the punch on a signature sandwich. The "Big M" was a double full-sized patty burger that came with cheese, chopped onion, lettuce, tomato and a relish sauce which debuted in 1966 - a full year before the introduction of the Big Mac.

Minute Man became part of the fabric of Arkansas food culture. Sadly, the chain dwindled over the years, to a single location that still operates today in El Dorado.

Or, at least, it had dwindled… until entrepreneur Perry Smith got involved, obtaining permission from the last Minute Man manager, Linda McGoogan. Smith has worked with a new team to bring the Minute Man legacy back into action, and in 2020 the first new Minute Man was opened in Jacksonville.

The spacious location north of Main Street retains much of the Minute Man charm, with large globe lights overhead and mementos of the original franchise run decking the walls. The scent of hot charcoal fills the space as burgers and Ark-Mex favorites are ordered, delivered and consumed.

The menu includes originals like the #2 Hickory Burger, the #6 Salad Burger, the Big M and of course those delicious, napalm hot Radar Range pies. It now includes rotisserie chicken, taquitos, and burritos which you can get with an excellent chimichurri sauce and guacamole!

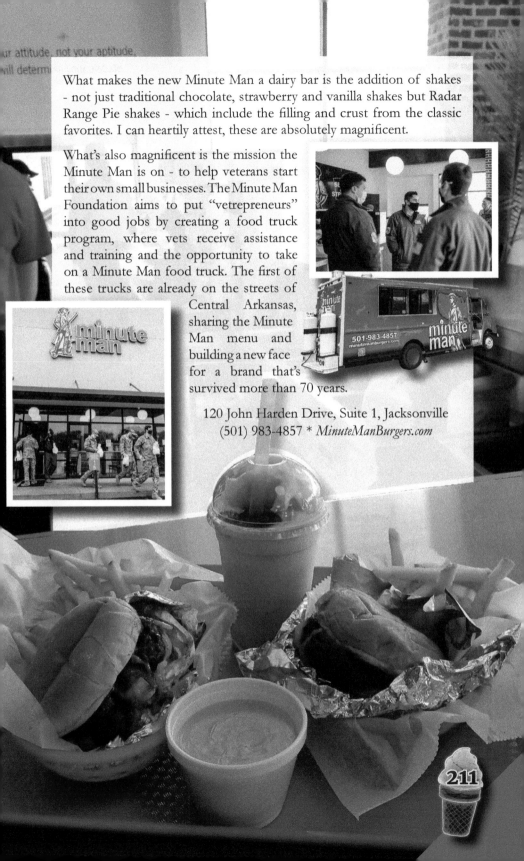

What makes the new Minute Man a dairy bar is the addition of shakes - not just traditional chocolate, strawberry and vanilla shakes but Radar Range Pie shakes - which include the filling and crust from the classic favorites. I can heartily attest, these are absolutely magnificent.

What's also magnificent is the mission the Minute Man is on - to help veterans start their own small businesses. The Minute Man Foundation aims to put "vetrepreneurs" into good jobs by creating a food truck program, where vets receive assistance and training and the opportunity to take on a Minute Man food truck. The first of these trucks are already on the streets of Central Arkansas, sharing the Minute Man menu and building a new face for a brand that's survived more than 70 years.

120 John Harden Drive, Suite 1, Jacksonville
(501) 983-4857 * *MinuteManBurgers.com*

MOJO'S DAIRY BAR

North Little Rock was once home to a host of dairy bars, like Freddie's on Broadway, Bray's Dairy Castle on 4th, the Davis Dairy Bar, The Spot on Camp Robinson under what is now I-40, and Kemp's on Pike Avenue. Today the city is home to three - The Original ScoopDog (see page 214), Wink's Dairy Bar (page 218), and Mojo's.

Formerly Andy's Dairy Freeze, which operated on the Old Conway Highway in the 1960s and 1970s, Mojo's still sits along MacArthur not far from Burns Park. It's grown over the years from a two window walk-up, adding a dining room and a patio and even a drive-thru.

Today it's known for great burgers and hot dogs, and a selection of milkshakes and sundaes. You can also get a basket of wings or a chef's salad. Calling ahead is recommended.

3801 MacArthur Drive, North Little Rock * (501) 753-4445

MORRILTON DRIVE INN RESTAURANT

A menu that has everything? That's what you'll find at this longstanding local favorite just south of Interstate 40. Originally opened in the 1970s, this family-sized restaurant boasts windows up front, a pull-up window at the side and a dining room large enough for a couple of high school sports teams to enjoy at one time.

The restaurant's original dairy bar menu of dogs, burgers, fries and shakes has been supplemented with chicken and barbecue dinners, catfish, tacos and burritos, breakfast selections and a pile of fried pies by the register.

One thing that sounds crazy but which is irresistibly good - try the chili steak, a breaded country fried steak sandwich treated like a chili cheeseburger. Probably bad for you, but oh so good.

1601 North Oak Street, Morrilton * (501) 354-8343

213

THE ORIGINAL
SCOOPDOG
old fashion
INC.

BANANA SPLIT

1 SCOOP   2 SCOOPS
CHOCOLATE   VANILLA

PINEAPPLE

STRAWBERRIES

BANANA

CHOCOLATE SYRUP

CARAMEL TOPPING

PECANS & PEANUTS

& A CHERRY

Gift Certificates
Available

pical

214

THE ORIGINAL SCOOPDOG

Not all dairy bars are burger stands. In North Little Rock, The Original ScoopDog offers the window service of the past, with frozen custard, city-themed hot dogs and canine-named fantastic sundaes.

"Scoop is the vanilla custard, the dogs are our hot dogs, and ScoopDog is a beagle," Joe Yanosick laughs, "or a wiener dog. Some people want to call him a wiener dog, but he's actually a beagle, and he was one of our dogs that passed away a few years ago.

"We started naming our sundaes after dogs, like the Poodle, the Golden Retriever, the Chocolate Lab - one of our customers, actually, came up with the Chocolate Lab. So we've named all the ice creams after a dog."

Joe and his wife, Kim, opened The Original ScoopDog along JFK Boulevard in North Little Rock in 1999 as Shake's Frozen Custard. After a falling-out with a business partner, the Yanosicks rebranded in 2009. The distinctive sign-covered building is a homegrown favorite for a city once known as Dogtown.

"My wife and my daughter paint most of the signs, but each sign represents a sundae or a type of concrete, and that's really about all there is to it," he continues, pointing out different hand-lettered and illustrated planks that adorn the outside of the 600 square foot facility. "Like, our banana split, our fudge brownie concrete. There's so many, and it's just very artistic. It gives this place a look like no other.

"We offer so many different items to choose from, so the signs represent different concretes and different sundaes, and we have that many selections here. There's not enough signs to represent what all we serve."

Instead of traditional dairy bar soft-serve or hand-scooped ice cream, honest-to-goodness frozen custard is the star here.

"We have a custard machine. My inspiration was Leon's Frozen Custard in Milwaukee, Wisconsin," Joe shares. "In 1929, he built our machine, and we have two machines, and we have one that we keep in our garage, just in case, but he doesn't even make these machines anymore. So our custard is made specifically for us from a dairy in Illinois, and we get the custard product in weekly. We run our custard fresh, probably every 15 to 30 minutes, we're turning our machine on to run our custard fresh."

The product ends up being extraordinarily creamy.

"I mean, you're not going to get a creamier ice cream dessert in Central Arkansas, because that custard is so thick, eggs, cream, and sugar. So that's what does separate it from a traditional, say, a soft serve that you might get at other places. It's a great product."

Joe invites me in to experience the custard-making process.

216

"So we pour our custard mix in here, and then there's a flow back here that determines how thick the custard will come out, and then, we'll be getting ready to start our machine in just a minute to run some fresh frozen custard."

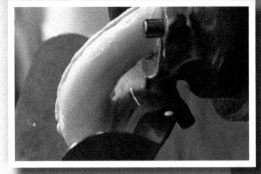

Even with the warning, I am not prepared for the sudden stirring of mechanical innards within the big metal case. It vibrates the air around it, silencing conversations. I feel my ears flatten against the side of my head as I compensate for not thinking to have a set of earplugs ready to go. Joe fiddles with knobs and levers.

"This machine's 20, 21 years old," he tells me, as I more lipread than hear what he's saying. "It'll take three to four minutes before it starts to firm up." I nod and watch for a few moments, noticing that his wife and one of his sons working today don't even glance up at the noise.

"So, see, as this gets colder, you could turn that flow up a little more to push more ice cream through, but, again, that flow is what controls how…" Joe demonstrates, opening up a chute. "if you run it too soft, you can't dump it over. It's gotta have enough liquid in there or otherwise it gets really loud."

I'm thinking to myself, louder than this?

"The blades are metal, so they maintain a perfect temperature through-out the cylinder. And then, we don't have to overwhip it, so therefore, it's a lot denser than products where they pump air or overwhip it. We're, like, the filet mignon," he chuckles, "of ice cream."

The custard extrudes above a bin inside a chest freezer, dropping each time Joe cuts it with a small metal paddle. When an order comes through the window for a cone, he expertly slides the paddle into a bin and grabs a single piece scoop, rolling the custard in three strokes into a perfect sphere, pressing it down into the cone, and passing it out the window without a break.

The machine is run several times a day. It takes about 20 minutes from putting in the mix and ingredients to finishing an extrusion. The Original ScoopDog makes vanilla and chocolate. All other flavors go on or in the concoctions when orders are placed.

"Chicago Dog and The Good Ole Beagle sundae, those are our two most popular items," he says as we step back outside. "Yeah, we get our hot dogs, and our buns are made for us in Chicago, and we get our deliveries twice a week, as a matter of fact, and we're the real deal. Pure beef, authentic Chicago-style hot dog. We use a skinless hot dog, but it still has the snap, and we're proud to serve a real Chicago Dog. You really can't get one, anywhere in the state now. We're about the only one left. Sports peppers, then you have the relish, yellow mustard, the pickles. We take pride in making our Chicago Dog the way you would get if you were in the street of Chicago.

"We've ended up going around the country and picking the most famous cities and the most famous hot dogs from the city. A Detroit Dog, mustard, chili, cheese, and onion, is authentic to Detroit. The Kansas

City-style hot dog is a Swiss cheese with sauerkraut, which is different. New York Dog is onions in a tomato-based sauce with spicy mustard on it. It's just like what you would get if you went to the street of New York. So, yes, all of our city dogs are authentic to the city that they represent.

"When we opened this store, people laughed 'cause they didn't know what frozen custard was, and we worked it when we got 10 cars a day, and now, we do 300, 400. Don't mess with hot dogs or frozen custard. Give 'em what they want."

My partner, Grav, and my best friend Leif brought my daughter Hunter to enjoy lunch at one of the picnic tables. "I like all of it, really," Hunter nods while downing a Detroit dog. "You know, all put together. It's just, it's great, it's lovely, it's beautiful." She gives a chef's kiss. This child is no stranger to food experiences, but it's this one that she chooses often.

"It's pure Americana," Leif shares while tackling the Sooie, a barbecue and bacon dog. "You know, you can pull in for a chili dog and a shake. It's definitely old school."

"People come here when they want a snack," Joe says. "They come here for lunch, come here for dinner, a late-night snack. So we're around the clock. We could probably open earlier and close later.

"I feel very, very blessed and lucky, to get to work with my children every day, and, again, see all the happy customers, it's a very rewarding experience. It's not easy owning a business. It isn't for everyone. You have your ups and downs, but I feel very lucky, very lucky. Great, great customers. We have the best."

Joe has laughed all through our interview, and it's obvious to me that he's happy as a clam. But I think he teared up just thinking about everything we've been talking about. He absentmindedly held his hand up to his chest for a moment, looking out over the patio.

"Just having a successful small business that makes customers happy is, that's everything."

5505 John F. Kennedy Boulevard, North Little Rock

(501) 753-5407 * *TheScoopDog.com*

SALEM DAIRY BAR

Lucy Begley has been the owner of the Salem Dairy Bar for more than 25 years. She has had customers that were teenagers when they first came by, who now bring their grandchildren by. She's seen it all.

"Mr. Baxley and Mrs. Baxley built it around 50 years ago," she shares with me. "We bought the property and building and stuff all from Mr. Baxley. Mae Miller ran it for years. Her niece still works for us. Willy Fletcher was working here when we bought it."

The Encyclopedia of Arkansas dates the establishment back to the 1960s, with construction attributed to Fulton Baxley. A former employee shares that its opening day was in 1961. John and Dee Baxley ran the shop in the 1970s, back when it was still called the Dairy Diner.

"So my husband was the one who wanted a restaurant. I didn't even like cooking," Lucy continues. "He was the one who wanted a restaurant, so we bought it. I worked in insurance before this and he was a welder, and neither one of us knew anything about running a restaurant. But we bought it, and it's been good to us! Our son's been raised in it. He's still working here right now, but just helping the new people."

Amidst the pandemic in 2020, Begley made the decision to pass along the business to a younger generation. "We have rented it out to one of my employees. She has taken it over and is gonna continue with the way it is."

Heather Queen is now the manager for the iconic institution. I've enjoyed chatting with her. If Lucy hadn't have said anything, I would not know anything's changed, thanks to the consistency of the menu and the quality of the food that comes out the window.

"The hamburgers are still the very same," Lucy says, "and cheeseburgers, hot dogs, chicken strips, chicken sandwiches. We've made a few changes through the years, added some things, dropped some things. We make our own fried pies. We make the dough and everything. We have a little ma- chine that presses 'em out where they're all uniform, and they're selling very well. Hot fudge - we just say chocolate, but it's hot fudge - peach and apple, and when I was here the other day, I found out they've added, they're trying out coconut now."

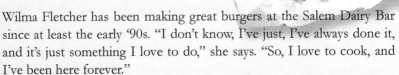

Wilma Fletcher has been making great burgers at the Salem Dairy Bar since at least the early '90s. "I don't know, I've just, I've always done it, and it's just something I love to do," she says. "So, I love to cook, and I've been here forever."

Turns out, this is Willie's 29th year running the grill. While other stations are manned with individuals who pull out onion rings, fries and fried items of different sorts, or man the window, Willie is in charge of her domain at the burger station. Each day she hand-pats hundreds of patties. They're kept in cold storage in a drawer below the grill. When an order comes in, she wipes down the griddle with a big cloth blotter, then pulls all the patties for the order.

In a single motion, she takes the patties from the drawer to the griddle top, sprinkles them with a salt and pepper blend, and flattens them with her spatula. She has had several dozen patties going at once on the griddle top, and she knows just when to flip and shake on spice on the other side. In-between, she stacks the condiments and vegetables on the top buns, then slides on the burger and bottom bun before sweeping the completed burger into a wax paper four corner wrap, inserting a toothpick, and sliding the finished order to the next person to put right into a bag.

One of the things that keeps people coming back is the big order of fluffy onion rings. The batter for the rings and the fried pickles consists of several things, including a special mix from Fordyce-based company HNO Blending. Lucy's son Brian Begley shares a secret about that batter.

"What we do is, whenever we put vanilla in the machine, vanilla ice cream, we'll leave about that much left in the bowl," he says, showing an amount between his finger and thumb. "We'll fill it up with water, and that'll be the sugar that, when we put it into the bowl, that's where the sugars come from. It's coming straight from the vanilla mix."

The result is a fluffy, somewhat sweet batter that makes these oversized, crunchy onion rings. I have yet to find an onion ring quite like this anywhere.

Most of the items, you can find on any dairy bar menu. It's about the quality of ingredients, the combination, the portion sizes. For instance, Salem Dairy Bar uses a large, long all-beef dog for its footlongs, and on request covers them with creamy housemade coleslaw, beefy chili and handfuls of shredded cheese - or relish, or anything you want.

Ice cream is always a big draw. Every person I spoke with the day we recorded video for the *Arkansas Dairy Bars* show told me they loved the sundaes - particularly the hot fudge sundae. Strawberry's another favorite, as are the magnificent snow cones that are most popular with teenagers from the local high school.

"The parking lot is usually full and what's weird is, probably 80 percent of our business is people calling their orders in and just coming and picking it up," Lucy tells me. "Most people don't ... now in the summertime people come out here and enjoy the weather. But we can be busy with orders and not have a car in the parking lot and then everybody pulls in and picks up their orders, and go and it starts again!"

The city of Benton and the Salem community to its northwest have all but merged over the past couple of decades, with the Salem Dairy Bar right at that meeting point. I can remember when it was truly out in the country. Today, it's not uncommon to see the lot completely full and cars parked down the dead-end street from the corner where the eatery sits. It's the epitome of a central Arkansas dairy bar, and is thriving.

"You've got people who will come here and say, 'Oh, my husband proposed to me here,' things like that," Lucy tells me. "It's not that stressful, really, except when everybody shows up at one time for their food, and then you have a dead spot for two hours, and then sometimes you get swamped and it gets frustrating. But it's not hard. You have to enjoy it."

6406 Congo Road, Benton * (501) 794-3929

223

SPRADLIN'S DAIRY DELIGHT

Back in 1957, Claude Spradlin started up a new business in England. Spradlin's wife had worked at a dairy bar in her hometown, and he figured that England needed one of its own. He was right. Spradlin's Dairy Delight caught on quickly, becoming the place to pick up a burger, a long hot dog or a Frito Chili Pie. A second Dairy Delight came along later. The sole location today still sports a lengthy oversized awning where customers can pull up under during inclement weather.

Spradlin's son, Claude Spradlin, Jr. took over in 1973 and still runs the business today. He has been part of the operation since the restaurant opened (he was seven at the time), and he took over the grill when he was 16. Spradlin says his dad actually came up with the Frito Chili Pie back when the restaurant started -- and that the folks at the Frito Lay Corporation actually sent him a letter thanking him for his contribution and the creation of the dish. It was sold in a paper boat for 15 cents -- a nickel for the Fritos and a dime for the chili -- and it was very popular.

Now, the general consensus is that Frito chili pie was first served in the 1960s by Theresa Hernandez at the Woolworth Five and Dime Store's lunch counter in Santa Fe, New Mexico. Others claim the mother of Frito founder Charles Elmer Doolin came up with the original -- and that Daisy Dean Doolin fashioned many Fritos dishes all the way back in the 1930s. According to the book **Frito Pie: Stories, Recipes and More** by Fritos creator's daughter Kaleta Doolin, a listing

for Fritos Chili Pie appeared in the 1949 menu for the Dallas Dietetic Association Convention, alongside Frito-Kettes (salmon croquettes with Fritos), Fritos Happy Landings and Fritos Eggplant Casserole.

The recipe itself was printed on Fritos bags back in 1962 and was credited to Nell Morris. However, this recipe called for layers of crushed Fritos alternating with chili, cheese and onions -- not the simpler Fritos covered with chili offered at Spradlin's. The advertising campaign built around the concoction was aimed at selling both Fritos and the new Frito brand chili just then available.

Claude Spradlin, Jr. plans to continue with the restaurant -- five days a week he gets to serve up food to friends and buddies who drop in for a bite to eat and to chat. Whether or not Spradlin's really is the original place where the Frito Chili Pie began, it's still a great little place to eat. Long dogs (foot long chili cheese dogs) are the most requested item on the menu, and cool cones are perfect during the summer.

24 North Main Street, England * (501) 842-2341.

225

THE WHIPPET FAMILY RESTAURANT AND DAIRY BAR

Located at the heart of Prattsville, this long-standing dairy bar has gone through a number of names and owners, from its opening as Lovoie's Drive In by the Shoptaw family in 1966 to its time as The Whippet Drive In in the 1970s while owned by Lester and Rema Gene Hollimon. In 1976, it was purchased by JW and Pauline Harrington, who eventually added a large dining room to the west side of the restaurant. It's been owned by the Henderson family since 1994.

The menu combines so many popular dairy bar specials, like griddle-fried hamburgers and crinkle cut fries, milk-

shakes and sundaes with family restaurant favorites such as the Whippet's famed catfish and hush puppies. Specials are available throughout the week, particularly a marvelous Tuesday steak night, which draws crowds from several counties around for gigantic steaks, baked potatoes, salad and rolls.

The restaurant also thrives on a number of desserts, notably one of the best local chocolate meringue pies and for its seasonal selection of Flywheel fried pies, the flavors of which come on a lightboard right when you walk inside.

9011 US Highway 270, Prattsville
(870) 699-4391
TheWhippet.com

WINK'S DAIRY BAR

Winford William "Wink" Walls opened the yellow two-window walk-up back in 1968 along Washington Street, on an avenue sandwiched between the bustle of Broadway and the Arkansas River. The façade has changed, but the restaurant, now under the auspices of Walls' daughter Diane McNutt, is essentially the same more than 50 years later.

Crowds form at lunch and dinner to enjoy the selection of burgers, sandwiches and plates that come through the window. The restaurant's reputation is built on its delectable tamales, which come in singles or multiples of three, smothered in chili and served with a handful of wrapped saltine crackers, used as scoops for the hot melange to be transported to the mouth.

Wink's does a lot of things really well. Chicken gizzards are sometimes offered, always served fresh fried. Pizza burgers, chicken fried steak sandwiches, even fried catfish are all expertly prepared.

While Wink's is indeed a full service dairy bar with shakes and sundaes, its pies are of particular repute. A selection of meringue-topped rounds are usually in full view on stands in the window, gone for the day once the tiers are empty. The sour cream chocolate cake is also divine.

2900 East Washington Avenue, North Little Rock * (501) 945-9025

YELLOW JACKET DRIVE IN

Originally opened in the early 50s as a Dairy Queen, then operating from the 60s to the mid-80s as Suttle's Dairy-Ette, this double-winged drive up dairy bar sits at the busiest intersection in Sheridan. Ordering is at the window at this bright blue edifice. The menu is packed with traditional dairy bar fare, plus things like pizza sticks and lots of fried vegetables.

Of note: the Double Hubcap Burger with Seasoned Fries, a massive two-hand burger. Ice cream is always on point, too. Try any milkshake with twist ice cream.

101 Rock Street, Sheridan * (870) 942-2486

Part of the reason dairy bars continue to exist is because of how they tie a community together. Many are named after the local high school mascot. Others bear the names of owners who become well known for their products and the atmosphere their restaurants exude. In some cases, these restaurants are the only locally owned and operated game in town.

They become beloved. Their continued presence in their communities are a stronghold against the winds of change. They're pockets of nostalgia held fast against the decades, a spot by the road where grandparents can share memories with their grandchildren, where first dates are made, where a young boy or girl has their first bite of cold ice cream, where a traveler can find a good bite to eat year after year.

Dairy bars matter, not just for what they sell and who runs them, but for their unique position as stand-alone eateries that remain open for business, even in the roughest of times. Though national chains and franchises have far encroached into their business model, these dairy bars have managed to keep on keeping on through the decades, serving all those who come to the window with a smile.

Restaurants have always come in a variety of shapes in sizes. A full service restaurant offers sit-down service, usually with wait staff inside. They range from high-end restaurants to local diners. Dairy bars, however, function differently. They are intrinsically linked with car culture. Ordering is at a window. The menu was written on a wall or marquee. The standard fare is burgers, hot dogs and other items that can be prepared somewhat quickly. And there is always ice cream.

When I started on this mission, to document Arkansas's dairy bar culture, I began by defining a dairy bar as a place that served ice cream and things other than ice cream, a permanent establishment that delivered its fine culinary offerings through a window. But there's more to it than that. A true dairy bar offers nostalgia... novelty... delicious and comforting food... prepared by dedicated individuals working with their families... whether those families are related by blood, by circumstances, by love or by choice. They are hallmarks of their communities. And as long as we remain hungry for neat eats, tasty treats, and good fellowship, Arkansas's dairy bars should continue to thrive.

RESTAURANTS BY ALPHA

ACKNOWLEDGMENTS

This book would not have been possible without the many people and organizations that have shown support for the research, travel, and compilation necessary to so thoroughly cover this topic.

My thanks to Jeff Dailey, Leif Hassell, Tracy Prince, Levi Agee, Kai Caddy, and Robb McCormick for the work done on *Arkansas Dairy Bars* for Arkansas PBS.

Appreciation is thusly given to the Arkansas PBS Foundation and the Arkansas PBS Network for commissioning the companion film to this book.

Special recognition should be given to the University of Arkansas Little Rock Special Collections, the Central Arkansas Library Service, the Arkansas State Archives, the Arkansas Department of Parks, Tourism and Heritage, Arkansas Tech University and the Arkansas Innovation Hub for assisting in the resources necessary to complete this book and to ensure its accuracy.

Much thanks to Sara Willis, for doing everything possible to convince me I wasn't crazy for pursuing this project.

Gratitude to my mother, Kitty Waldon, and my daughter, Hunter Robinson, for putting up with the constant, rigorous work this endeavor entailed.

And as always, this project could not have been completed without my partner, Grav Weldon, who not only provided me the emotional support, cooked meals, handled household tasks and literally wrangled cats, but who also stepped in as colorist on the show, proofreading editor and major general of the army of "you can do this" to make sure I not only managed to complete this book but also not lose what's left of my sanity. You have my love, patience and gratitude.

Kat Robinson is Arkansas's food historian and most enthusiastic road warrior. The Little Rock-based author is the host of the Emmy-nominated documentary *Make Room For Pie; A Delicious Slice of The Natural State* and the Arkansas PBS show *Home Cooking with Kat and Friends*, as well as the host and producer of the 2021 documentary *Arkansas Dairy Bars: Neat Eats and Cool Treats*. She is a member of the Arkansas Food Hall of Fame committee, a co-chair of the Arkansas Pie Festival, and the Arkansas fellow to the National Food and Beverage Museum.

She has written eleven books on food, most notably *Arkansas Food: The A to Z of Eating in The Natural State*, an alphabetic guide to the dishes, delights and food traditions that define her home state. Two of her more recent travel guides, *101 Things to Eat in Arkansas Before You Die* and *102 More Things to Eat in Arkansas Before You Die* define the state's most iconic and trusted eateries. Robinson's *Another Slice of Arkansas Pie: A Guide to the Best Restaurants, Bakeries, Truck Stops and Food Trucks for Delectable Bites in The Natural State* outlines more than 400 places to find the dessert, an extraordinary accomplishment that took thousands of miles, hundreds of hours and so many bites to properly document and catalogue.

She shares her personal life experiences in *A Bite of Arkansas: A Cookbook of Natural State Delights*, the 2020 memoir and cookbook which offers 140 recipes made by and photographed herself. She also recently edited and contributed to the collection *43 Tables: An Internet Community Dines During Quarantine*.

In addition to this work, the nostalgic *Arkansas Dairy Bars: Neat Eats and Cool Treats*, the companion book for the Arkansas PBS television special of the same name, Robinson's other 2021 work, *Arkansas Cookery: Retro Recipes from The Natural State*. In the book, she examines mid-century cookbooks from all over Arkansas. Robinson's collection of more than 400 20th century cookbooks and research into common threads of shared recipes, cooking methods and flavors of the era has been brought together for this lovingly photographed collection of the foods previous generations brought to the table. The recipes, redacted and cooked with period methods at The Writer's Colony at Dairy Hollow in Eureka Springs, were all shot on location. The lushly illustrated book will be released in fall 2021.

Kat Robinson's work has appeared in regional and national publications including *Food Network, Forbes Travel Guide, Serious Eats*, and *AAA Magazines*, among others. Her expertise in food research and Arkansas restaurants has been cited by *Saveur, Eater, USA Today, The Wall Street Journal, The Outline*, and the Southern Foodways Alliance's *Gravy* podcast, for her skills and talents related to food research and documentation.

Her efforts have been celebrated in articles by *Arkansas Good Roads, Arkansas Business, 501 Life Magazine*, the *Northwest Arkansas Democrat-Gazette* and the *Arkansas Democrat-Gazette*. She has served as the keynote speaker for the South Arkansas Literary Festival and the Arkansas Library Association Conference and has spoken at the Six Bridges Literary Festival, Eureka Springs Books in Bloom and the Fayetteville True Lit Festival.

While she writes on food and travel subjects throughout the United States, she is best known for her ever-expanding knowledge of Arkansas food history and restaurant culture, all of which she explores on her 1200+ article website, *TieDyeTravels.com*.

Robinson's journeys across Arkansas have earned her the title "road warrior," "traveling pie lady," and probably some minor epithets. Few have spent as much time exploring The Natural State, or researching its cuisine. "The Girl in the Hat" has been sighted in every one of Arkansas's 75 counties, oftentimes sliding behind a menu or peeking into a kitchen.

Kat lives with daughter Hunter and partner Grav Weldon in Little Rock.

You can contact the author at *kat@tiedyetravels.com* with questions or correspondence - or, of course, recommendations on great recipes and wonderful places to eat in Arkansas.

Books by Kat Robinson

Arkansas Pie:
A Delicious Slice of the Natural State
History Press, 2012

Classic Eateries of the Ozarks
and Arkansas River Valley
History Press, 2013

Classic Eateries of the Arkansas Delta
History Press, 2014

Another Slice of Arkansas Pie: A Guide to the
Best Restaurants, Bakeries, Truck Stops and Food
Trucks for Delectable Bites in The Natural State
Tonti Press, 2018

Arkansas Food:
The A to Z of Eating in The Natural State
Tonti Press, 2018

101 Things to Eat in Arkansas Before You Die
Tonti Press, 2019

102 More Things to Eat in Arkansas
Before You Die
Tonti Press, 2019

43 Tables:
An Internet Community Cooks During Quarantine
Tonti Press, 2020

A Bite of Arkansas:
A Cookbook of Natural State Delights
Tonti Press, 2020

This book:
Arkansas Dairy Bars: Neat Eats and Cool Treats
Tonti Press, 2021

And next:
Arkansas Cookery:
Retro Recipes from The Natural State
Tonti Press, 2021

NOTES